G   Thomas OBE is the winner of the 2018 Tour de
    a double Olympic gold medallist and multiple world
    ion who has been indispensable part of Team Sky
   s inception. A Tour de France veteran, he had both
   ted the entire race with a fractured pelvis and been
   ial in piloting Chris Froome to the yellow jersey
   le times before his own win.

   of the most popular men in the peloton, he has
   d and contributed from the inside as British cycling
   n transformed over the past decade. In 2014 he won
   onwealth road race gold in Glasgow and was voted
   ales Sport Personality of the Year. In 2015 he became
    British rider to win the E3 Harelbeke and in 2016
   Paris–Nice. Having worn the Tour de France leader's
   jersey in 2017, 2018 saw him first win the Critérium
   ohiné and then, a few months later, become only the
   iton in history to take overall victory at the Tour
   le was subsequently voted BBC Sports Personality
   ear, beating Lewis Hamilton and Harry Kane in the
   ote.

Also by Geraint Thomas

The World of Cycling According to G

GERAINT THOMAS

THE
TOUR
ACCORDING
TO G

Written with Tom Fordyce

Quercus

First published in Great Britain in 2018 by Quercus.
This paperback edition published in 2019 by

Quercus Editions Ltd
Carmelite House
50 Victoria Embankment
London EC4Y 0DZ

An Hachette UK company

A CIP catalogue record for this book is available
from the British Library

PB ISBN 978 1 78747 905 0
Ebook ISBN 978 1 78747 904 3

10 9 8 7 6 5 4 3 2 1

Typeset by CC Book Production
Printed and bound in Great Britain by Clays Ltd, Elcograf S.p.A.

For all the dreamers young and old.
Dream big. Keep going. With hard work,
anything is possible.

Contents

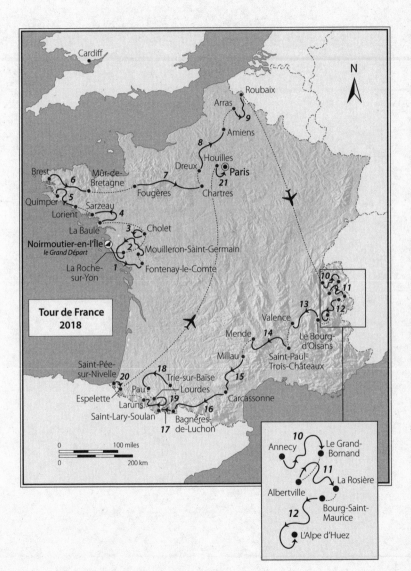

Chapter One

The Crash and the Fall

When you crash the road comes up at you fast. When you crash there is no good way to fall. When you crash your body takes the first impact but your mind suffers for much longer.

The 2017 Tour de France. I am in second place in the general classification, only my Sky teammate Chris Froome ahead of me. I have been in the yellow jersey, winning the prologue in the rain of Düsseldorf and holding on to it for four more days, and I am within touching distance of it still. The podium in Paris is no longer a teenage dream. I have never finished in the top ten at a Tour, my role repeatedly to work for my leader Froome and protect him from the race's cruel tests rather than spend my energies on my own ambitions. One year, I hope, it might be different. One year, by shepherding Froome, I might find myself with him all the way to the Champs-Élysées.

Already there have been crashes. Alejandro Valverde, the consistently competitive Spaniard, broke his kneecap after going down on a slippery corner on that Saturday afternoon prologue. I have hit the deck three times in the first eight stages, but all of the crashes were minor ones, all of them ones I could stand back up from and remount my bike.

Stage 9, from Nantua in the Jura mountains to Chambery, 181 twisting, climbing kilometres away. Seven cols to be summited, more than 4,500 vertical metres to suck from the legs. We are on the Col de la Biche, the first *hors catégorie* climb of the race, meaning that it is too steep and too tough for all but the insane and elite to attempt. 10.5km in length, an average gradient of 9%. You click into your smallest gear and you begin to work and you feel your legs burn and your heart jumping against your skin.

It starts to rain. A road already lumpy in places and slippery slick in others becomes more treacherous with every cold, wet minute. We are riding at the front of the peloton, a thin white line of Sky jerseys, trying to control the pace, trying to keep attacks at bay and keep tight our hold on the race. Luke Rowe, my old friend and fellow graduate of the Maindy Flyers cycling club in Cardiff, is pacing us at the front. Towards the summit, I'm in fifth or sixth place, uncomfortable but in control, wanting the climb to end but relishing its tests too.

An acceleration coming round outside us. The brown, white and pale blue jerseys of the French team AG2R, working for their team leader Romain Bardet, boyish face but a constant danger in these high mountains. A sprint for the top, for the points the summit brings for those chasing the King of the Mountains classification, but there are no points left, the breakaway has mopped all those up. I stand on the pedals and get out of the saddle, but by the time we crest the top and see the road dropping away in front of us I am back in ninth. Everyone wants to be as far forward as possible to limit the chance of crashing, but there is no real need for this stress. We create it ourselves. If a team attacks down this descent, with so far still to race, are they going to keep going all day and hold that advantage? Not a chance. You'd give them 200/1 odds. So why don't we all just stay where we are and ride down the descent like we would in training? Oh, it's the Tour, you have to stress, right? It only takes one team to start kicking it off, and that leaves you a cruel choice: stay relaxed and drift back, or join in. You have to join in.

110km left; so far my position is not a major issue for the final standings, but on this twisty, narrow descent, you never know what could change. The further back you are, the more you are forced to react to the desires and flaws of others rather than cutting your own lines. The rider in front of you brakes, you have to brake. The guy three riders up goes wide on one corner and then cuts across the next one, you have to scrub off speed to keep from touching wheels, and when you scrub off speed you have to work hard to get it back, accelerating out of the corner to stop the invisible length of elastic that holds this line of riders from snapping rather than stretching.

All of us know this. So a race within a stage within the race begins – each rider fighting for each additional position, taking outlandish risks, brushing elbows and shouting insults and angry instructions. You want to take it easier but you understand that as soon as you do then others will come past you. You have to fight just to stay where you are. You have to match those risks or else you will go backwards while going forwards at an eye-watering speed. Sixty miles from the finish, almost two weeks to Paris, and we are racing flat out and wild-eyed.

In this situation I like to give myself a bit of space, a couple of bike lengths. At 50kph and faster, it could make the difference between crashing or staying up. The only problem is that the guys behind you will see this as weakness. 'He's losing the wheel. Shit, I need to get past him.' Boys, chill.

Glimpses of a dark jersey with white flash in the corner of my vision. A rider behind me, trying to get past when there is no room. Overlapping his front wheel with my back wheel, that's where danger lies – a slight twitch either way from one of us and the tyres will touch and the bikes will buck and one of us, probably both, will be down.

I glance back. Rafał Majka, the Polish climber, Bora-Hansgrohe. Aquamarine helmet, white-framed mirrored sunglasses. Another corner, Majka still all over the back of me. It triggers memories of the Tour in 2015, sixteenth stage, on another technical descent, when Warren Barguil came into a right-hander way too hot and clattered into my torso. I saved him, kept him upright. But he sent me sideways, Mario Kart-style, first into a telegraph pole with my head and then down into a ravine.

I'll let Majka past. Too much to risk at this point, too much to lose.

Majka comes past. A breath of relief. Time to settle, to find serenity at 70kph.

Round a right-hander. Trees on the slopes above, patches of silvery light on the road where the water has settled, darker patches where the surface is more porous and the rain has soaked in. I'm letting no one else past now. One is enough. No more danger. No more madness. Sod the buffer, I'm all in.

Round the bend and Majka is down on the road in front of me. One moment I have that image frozen in my mind and the next my bike is on his and the road is slamming me from the side. Squealing rubber and shouts and the sound of carbon breaking and another body cracking and squishing on the tarmac and then a sudden silence.

You crash and you get back to your feet. You look for your bike and your glasses and you jump back on. You chase to get back amongst the noise and the living, and you worry about the injuries later. It is the seconds bleeding away that scare you, not the sliced knees and elbows or the skin grated off your shoulder and backside. Get back on and ride.

Except this time, I can't get up. Something doesn't feel right. I can roll into a sitting position but I can't put any weight through my right arm. I don't know what happened to Majka but I can see him a few yards back up the road, jersey shredded across his stomach and chest, and I can see Matteo Trentin, the Italian who rides in the blue of Quick-Step, on the road as well.

A familiar voice in my ear. It is Bernie Eisel, the Austrian who used to ride with me at Sky, one of the good guys. He is with Dimension Data now, and he didn't have to stop, but he has.

'G. Are you okay?'

'Yeah, yeah. You go ahead. Don't wait for me.'

A snap as Bernie clicks his cleat back into his pedal, and away he goes. A car screeching to a halt behind me, the voice of team doctor Juan Mercadel, a man we call Jimmy. He sits me up and checks my head and neck, my back, my shoulders. On the right-hand side there is both numbness and pain.

'G. Your collarbone. I think it's broken.'

You don't race your bike to hear these things. I have ridden an entire Tour with a fractured pelvis, after crashing right at the start of the 2013 race. I had to be lifted onto my bike each morning, because I couldn't lift my leg high enough to get it over the crossbar. You don't race because it makes sense. You are stubborn where others are weak, remorseless where others crumble. You know what a broken collarbone means. It's the end of the Tour. It's another chance gone. Another year older, a team leader left without his lieutenant with more than half the race still to come.

'It can't be. It's fine.'

'G. Sorry. It's broken.'

I look up. Sky mechanic Gary Blem has my bike. He has re-seated the chain, checked the brakes. It is ready to ride even if I am not.

'I'm going to ride. Just to make sure.'

Jimmy is shaking his head at me and giving Gary a look. Gary looks sad and resigned but powerless too. 'The second car will stay with him, Jimmy. We won't leave him.'

My sunglasses? They are in pieces on the road, where

the other team cars have driven over them. Another pair gone, another Tour? No, not yet. Clipping in. Holding the handlebars gingerly, starting to pick up speed on the descent. Froome and Bardet and those around them are way ahead, gone into the wet distance, but this is no longer about hanging on to second place. It's hoping for a miracle. It's wanting to be part of this race more than anything else in the world, not watching it like a civilian, passive, distant.

My left foot feels loose. I look down and see that the buckle has come undone in the crash. I reach down with my left hand to fasten it. Now only my right hand is on the bars, and it is like someone has flicked a cruel switch. Pain stabs through that shoulder, across my back, into my left shoulder and down both arms. I can't hold on. I come back upright and try to ride with my left hand only, but my entire upper body is now on fire, the pain jabbing up my neck and into my head. This isn't okay. This isn't going away.

A Sky car pulls up alongside me. Servais, the second DS – *directeur sportif* – is leaning out of the window. His face is all concern and foreboding.

'G. You're going to stop then?'

I tell him I'm going to be okay, knowing that this is a lie, knowing that Servais knows it's a lie. Thirty seconds of riding, the pain ramping up through the gears. Twenty seconds of riding, each breath in hurting. Another glance at Jimmy. Ten seconds more.

A squeeze on the brakes, gently steering to the dark green verge. Rain in the air. Head down low.

It's over.

The race doctor pulls up in the ambulance and makes his own assessment. The diagnosis is the same.

It hits you as you sit in the race ambulance. The adrenaline wearing off, the pain gripping tight. Your jersey tattered and stained dark with gravel and mud, your hair plastered to your face. Bib-shorts damp with sweat and rain.

I still have my team radio in my pocket, the earpiece dangling loose. I can hear our lead DS Nico Portal talking to the riders up the road. It is like eavesdropping on a private party, sitting on the steps outside the greatest nightclub in the world. You were in there, at the centre of it all, the noise, the danger, the excitement, the feeling of leanness and speed and power. And now you are gone, banished, left on the outside with all the others who couldn't handle it, who didn't train five hours a day and starve themselves so that their cheekbones stuck out and their faces recessed away so much that their noses and eyes and ears seemed to grow.

By the side of the road is Marko, one of the team soigneurs. They are the uncomplaining worker bees of the unit, washing clothes, giving massages, tidying up our messes. He is there on the climb because he has been handing out drinking bottles to the boys who have already flashed through. He sits beside me and he says nothing, because he understands what I am going through. The ambulance, all calm and white interior, my head a thumping mess of disbelief, distress and remorse. One thought on a loop, holding off all the others: this better fucking be broken now. If I've stopped and I could have been patched up, if I could have ridden just another few miles to see if it settled, if I could have somehow got through to the end of the day and seen how it might have been in the morning . . .

At the team hotel I find out I am not the only one. It has been a demolition derby of a stage, skinny bodies left scattered across the Jura mountains. Eleven men down in total, including Manuele Mori with a dislocated shoulder and punctured lung, Robert Gesink with a broken vertebra, and Jesús Herrada with a dislocated kneecap. Then there is Richie Porte, for so long a teammate at Sky, now switched to BMC to see if he has what it takes to win big outside our safe cocoon. Porte has gone down on the final descent of the day, off the Mont du Chat, 95km further through the stage, up above the town of Aix-les-Bains. I watch the footage of his crash – his back wheel locking up as he went into a series of S-bends too fast, his front wheel slipping off the left-hand side of the road, his bike going down and slamming him into the rocks on the opposite side. He is stretchered off the mountain in a red neck brace, broken clavicle, fractured pelvis. Dan Martin, the Irishman riding for Quick-Step, went down over him, picked himself up, continued on the descent and immediately crashed again. He will only discover upon finishing the Tour in Paris that he has broken two vertebrae in his back too.

The team put me on a private jet to take me home. The Easyjet flight is an hour and a half away; I have lots of luggage, including – having been in yellow – several fluffy toy lions, the traditional daily gift for the race leader from the Tour organisers, ASO. I'm grateful for all that, and I'd rather be at home than in a team hotel that's been left like a budget ghost-town after all have moved on to the next stage and next host town, but it is when you are at home that it really hits you. I sit on the sofa, trussed up, eating almost normally again after those months of denial and privation, and I feel sore and fat. I know the boys will be gutted for me. I know too that tomorrow they will forget, that the race will move on and attention will focus on the next challenge, the next climb and attack. You are an essential cog in the machine until you are gone, and when you are gone, you understand that while appreciated, you are also disposable. The machine marches on without you. The Tour never looks back, only forward. There is no rear-view mirror on a bike.

You race your bike, you crash your bike. I have gone down in Europe, in South America, in Australia. I have crashed on roads and in velodromes. I have fallen off mountains and into trees.

You tell yourself you're not cursed. It happens to all of us. It is an occupational hazard. Crashing during a time trial at Tirreno-Adriatico, over a barrier and bouncing down a rocky slope, breaking my pelvis and scaphoid. Crashing during a bunch sprint finish at the Tour Down Under in 2011, leading out my teammate Ben Swift, taken out as two other riders tried to get through a gap only big enough for one. Rupturing my spleen riding in Sydney, one month after graduating from the junior ranks, landing on top of the stem of my handlebars, not a mark on the skin but deep trauma underneath.

When you're fresh-faced and your career is ahead of you, you bounce well both physically and mentally. You recover fast and you always have another target to focus on. The pain is temporary, the future before you.

When you creep past thirty years old, you are a better rider and a wiser one too. You have seen the churn of top riders, the speed with which the old kings are dethroned and the new kids come through. You have watched friends and rivals win the biggest prizes and seen what it has done for their reputation and sense of satisfaction.

You understand that chances have to be taken, that form can take an age to find. When I went to the Giro d'Italia in May 2017, two months before the Tour and the ordeal on the Col de la Biche, it was the culmination of six months of the most intense training of my life. For the first time with Sky I was a team leader. No Froomey, not at the Giro. Seven of the other eight riders in black were the supporting cast this time; Mikel Landa and I were the twin arrowheads at the front.

And I was in form. Tim Kerrison, Team Sky's coach, is a genius of periodisation, of pushing you in training and then easing off in a way that can get you to peak not just for the start of a three-week Grand Tour but for the part of that race that you will need it the most. I won the Tour of the Alps across five days in mid-April, beating the charismatic Frenchman Thibaut Pinot, taking the third stage and then repelling every attack Pinot launched at me on the final day. At Tirreno-Adriatico, the seven-day stage race in March, I had won the second stage, attacking on the sort of steep climb I would encounter at the Giro.

I have always been a rider who could compete across the styles and disciplines. Winner of Junior Paris–Roubaix over the famous cobbles in the far north-east of France, of two Olympic gold medals as part of the Great Britain team pursuit quartet on the track, holding off Alberto Contador and Porte to win the Paris–Nice stage race. The criticism from some on the outside was that I was tilting at the wrong titles – that I should be focused purely on the one-day Classics, where a man with my six-foot frame would have the strength and power, rather than on the general classification of the Grand Tours. I had won E3 Harelbeke, the first of the spring cobbled Classics, in 2015, and come third at the next, Gent–Wevelgem. I loved those bleak, windy April days in the flatlands of France and Belgium, but I knew there was more within me.

And so I took my motivation from that. I'm going to show you what I can do. I'm going to prove you all wrong.

Across the first eight days of the Giro, I felt wonderful. Once again I was second in the overall contest, hunting down what would have been the biggest and most beautiful prize of my career, the famous *maglia rosa*. I'd never felt such form. No danger and no struggles on the first summit finish up Mt Etna, into a stiff headwind. Looking forward to testing my legs on the infamous Blockhaus climb, the brutal crescendo to 149km from Montenero di Bisaccia.

All of us rivals were at the front of the lead group as we accelerated towards the bottom of the climb, everyone sprinting for position so that they could cover attacks or launch their own, rather than being blocked and buried in the chaos of the pack further back. Me sixth from the front, blind to the road in front but trusting the rider in front as always, and the *carabinieri* to have cleared the traffic from our path.

Instead it was the *carabinieri* who stood in the way. One lone police motorbike rider, parked up by the side of the road just around a bend, directly in the path of the unsuspecting express train of cyclists coming his way. You don't see him when you're travelling at that speed and you have no chance of avoiding him.

Wilco Kelderman, the Dutchman in the black and white of Team Sunweb, was on the left-hand side of the road. He didn't stand a chance. Bang. Down. Into the next man, into me.

No reaction time at all. One instant you're following the wheel and you're getting ready for the climb and thinking about holding your position. The next thing you know, you've been clattered from the blind side and you're mid-air falling and the road has rushed up to meet you once again, and it's 'what the hell happened' and 'how am I on the floor?'

I may have partly landed on a bike as well. My teammate Landa was down outside me and Britain's Adam Yates was amongst us in the tangle of metal and rubber and limbs. I landed on my right shoulder for sure. A blitz of excruciating pain. Dislocated, far more painful in that horrible winded moment than the snapped collarbone.

The doctor alongside me, taking the weight off it. I felt it pop back in. Sudden blissful relief. I felt like a million dollars. Everyone, I'm sweet! I'm fine, we're going again!

Except I wasn't. I lost five minutes to Nairo Quintana that day but finished the stage. I rode a good time trial the following day, somehow, and came in second behind Tom Dumoulin. The shoulder was getting worse, however, and so was my knee. Lost time on stage 11, a sprinters' finish that really shouldn't have tested me, more again on stage 12. It sank in again on those long lonely miles before I abandoned on the night of the 13th: this is it. This isn't happening. This isn't going to happen this year.

I was standing outside the kitchen truck with Sky principal Dave Brailsford when the decision was made. Look, I haven't just come here to ride, have I? This isn't the old days, when it was about somehow battling through, no matter where you finished. I came here to win this race, or to at least stand on the final podium. This was never about limping to Milan. Dave agreed. Go home. Recover. Get ready to help Froomey at the Tour. And so that was the call we made.

The physical injuries healed fast but the scarring was deeper. The Giro was my big hit. I was atop the pyramid rather than the solid block one line down. I could make sense of Majka's fall. Racing accidents happen. He hadn't intentionally crashed in front of me. He was descending to win. But a police motorbike sticking out into the road after a blind corner? That should never happen. That's ridiculous. At least at the Tour I had won a stage and worn the yellow jersey. I had those days in the lead and those cuddly toy lions to take home. Italy left me with nothing, when I had been ready to prove to the cynics that I had everything. Christmas was cancelled.

I flew to the north of England for treatment with the Manchester City medical team. From there, shoulder and knee patched up, it was home to Monaco. I had no idea how the Giro was progressing and no desire to find out. I watched none of it. People around me were talking about it, about the dramatic final few days, about the ascendancy of Dumoulin. The day Tom sealed it in the time trial on the final Saturday, a few of us went over to Aussie rider Caleb Ewan's place for a barbecue. They had the race on the television. I sat on the balcony for most of it, desperate not to see it.

I dealt with it like a typical bloke: not talking about it, going into my own little world, being quiet when others are animated, running the accident over and over again in my head. After the Tour I had been to see the specialist about my shoulder. Driving home, I had got stuck at a set of traffic lights. I looked around me at the humdrum scenes, the red lights and the red faces. I couldn't believe I was sat here at a crossroads in the centre of Cardiff when I should have been racing in the Alps.

My wife Sara helped me through it as always. She had barely been able to watch those races, thinking herself the curse, understanding what the consequences were for my career and my character. I have always had belief but she buttressed it in those fragile moments. You're too good for it not to happen. Just keep doing the right thing. Put yourself in the right place and it will happen.

She brought a different type of normality. Not the dull emptiness of being unable to race, but the perspective that cycling is not the entire world. Her best friends Cadi, Ffion and Sian had arranged to come out to our flat in Monaco during the Tour, while I was supposed to be away across the border in France. Instead I gate-crashed their girls' holiday, and it was great – normal nights out, everyone in a good mood, not a word of cycling talk. Wales rugby winger George North was on holiday in Cannes with his partner Becky James so they came out for a night. George, however, failed spectacularly to match my drinking and retired to bed at an hour when I was still going strong. The hangover was stiff but so was the pride of outlasting a man of 6ft 4ins and 17 stone. Because my two big race targets had gone, I could recover the next day on the beach with an ice-cream. Racing cyclists do not eat ice-cream.

You don't want to be defined by crashes. You do not want to be a rider that others say is unlucky. Better to be called fortunate on the top step of the podium than unlucky in the ambulance. I have never thought I was cursed. I try to move on. Recover, look forward, always another race in the sights.

It's most difficult when you blame yourself. It was Majka's crash at the Tour. The policeman and his bike at the Giro. But at the Olympic road race in Rio in 2016, it was me. It was all down to me.

You have to be greedy as an elite sportsman. I had won those two Olympic golds on the track in the pursuit quartet but I wanted three. The road race is also about being part of a team; you don't find yourself in a good position going into the finale unless your teammates have helped control the pace and the breaks and protected you from the wind, but you cross the finish line alone. It was the first major final of those Games. It could have been the first British gold of what turned out to be a torrent.

And I was right there. My old mate Ian Stannard and Steve Cummings had done a fantastic job closing the gaps on the breaks; after almost 5,000m of climbing and multiple descents of the Vista Chinesa I was on the final drop and the final corner, Majka ahead of me and me confident I could close the gap. And on that final corner, I just went in a touch too fast, trying to close that gap in front too quickly and keep open the gap behind to Greg Van Avermaet, and I totally misjudged it. Way too far left rather than cutting a safe line through the middle of the corner, I jammed the brakes too hard and my back wheel skidded out on a road already rough and greasy with rain. That back wheel went into the gutter by a couple of millimetres, and down I went.

I remounted but the chance was gone. Van Avermaet was past me, and with him Jakob Fuglsang. Both would catch Majka before the finish along Rio's Copacabana. Van Avermaet would win the sprint, and I would trail home eleventh, jersey ripped, blood seeping through the mesh fabric on my back and elbows.

I knew I could have caught Majka. Maybe Greg would still have caught me. Had it come down to a sprint for the line you would have fancied him. Maybe I was lucky to be that far up, after Vincenzo Nibali and Sergio Henao had crashed themselves at the top of that final descent.

Maybe I would have launched my attack early had I

been there with Van Avermaet, used my pursuit strength to go long and burn them off. I was feeling great. My legs, after all that work from Stannard and Cummings, having stretched away from Chris Froome and Adam Yates, were fresh enough.

Instead, my mistake cost me the chance to find out. I tried to tell myself not to think about where it happened. Last corner or first corner, it doesn't matter. A crash is a crash. There were so many scenarios that could have played out that you should accept that what's done is done. Think of the next race. Just get over it.

Yet I knew it was the one that got away. Thinking of the next goal didn't help; the Olympics only come round once every four years. It's rare and special. 237.5km of climbing and cobbles and attacks and attrition, and I was 10km from the flat and the finish. Even now I think about Rio.

And I fight the idea that I'm somehow cursed. Rio, the Giro, the Tour, all ended by crashes, but I will not be defined by them. As 2018 came round, and with it the talk that my chances had gone, that I would never have that extra five or ten per cent that a Grand Tour winner needs, I drew it all in as motivation.

I don't say these things in public. In interviews I'm chilled. I don't shout about what I can do or where I'm going next. I'm not a sprinter or a boxer. I don't care about hype, only about the racing.

It doesn't mean I lack ambition or motivation. It doesn't mean I don't really care. It means I do an extra hour of training after already long and punishing days on Mount

Teide in Tenerife when the rest of the boys go back to the hotel for massages and food. Working my body to exhaustion and then being unable to feed it and reward it as others would. Going to sleep hungry and waking up so tired I have to let gravity do the legwork to get me out of bed.

There is nothing better than proving the doubters wrong. I don't read a lot of reports because you soon start disagreeing with them and they can stay on your mind. I just hear one or two things and think, right, okay, cool, shut up, I'll show you.

Before our two Olympic finals on the track, anxiety and doubt were constantly knocking on the door. My teammate Ed Clancy, the great engine of that world-record-breaking quartet, used to be beset by nerves. 'What if the Australian team ride an absolute blinder? What if I go out too fast and we blow it?' Through our tribulations and successes, we developed a collective attitude to get us through. Don't worry about other teams and other riders. Control what you can control. Trust in your training and the instincts it has honed.

So I did, as 2017 became 2018. It wasn't easy. I had been in the best shape of my life for no reward. The dangerous little thought worming round my head was this: will I ever get in that sort of shape again? It's so rare ... The defence I used against it was unyielding logic. Of course I'll be in this shape again, it's not luck that I've got here. I know how I got into that shape, the work I did, the miles I climbed, the weight I shed. I just commit like that again and get in that shape. That's all I can do. Next year somebody else might be super strong. I might have more bad luck. I can't control either. Obsess only about myself.

I told myself 2017 was one ill-fated year. I couldn't be unlucky all the time. Keep doing the right thing. Find the best form possible. Ride in the right place in the peloton.

It will happen eventually. One year, one race, I will show them.

Sara Thomas

The Giro aftermath in 2017 was the worst one, a massive, massive low. At the Tour, Geraint was going well but he knew he wasn't like he was for the Giro.

He doesn't normally go on about how good he's feeling. He keeps it all in. I can work it out for myself now, I know the signs. If he's happy and chatty it's going well, if he's quiet and reserved we've got some work to do. Before the Giro, he kept telling me the same thing: 'I feel so good.' And then how the crash happened – it would have been easier to take if he did something wrong, but it was just completely out of the blue.

You don't want to be that person who says, 'It's only a bike race.' Even though you know it is and there's so much more going on. You can't. It is a bike race, but it is so much more as well. I think he thought, this is my one big chance, I don't know if I'm going to get this again.

What really got to him was all the 'Geraint crashes again' stuff. He pretends he doesn't care but he really does. There's not much you can do when the person in front of you goes down. It winds him up. He's quite logical so when he gets emotional that's how I know he's really hurt.

He goes quiet. So quiet. He was really sad for a while

after that, and part of me knew I just had to let him be sad. I could suggest a holiday, try to get away to take his mind off it, but his knee was sore and he wouldn't have been able to enjoy it.

You feel a bit helpless, because there's nothing you can do to make it better, and that's tough. The Giro goes on and you know someone has to win the race, but you kind of don't want anyone to win it. Geraint likes Tom Dumoulin, but equally Tom's victory made it worse, because he's a Geraint-style rider. Bar the accident, he knew he was good enough.

Chapter Two

Grand Départ

Early July, the west of France. Brits come to the Vendée to kick back on the beaches, to camp in the pine forests that run down the coast, to sit out in the cafés of Les Sables-d'Olonne and Saint-Jean-de-Monts.

Us? We come here to race, and we come here reduced. You know you are ready for the Tour de France when you pull on your belt and find you need to make another hole, when you look down at your stomach to see two big veins sticking out at the bottom.

It's as hard on the head as the body. You want to drop the weight as quickly as you would a sprinter on a climb, but it takes months. In training camps and at races, our chef makes the food and our team nutritionist tells us how much we can put on our plates. When neither is there, you need help. So we WhatsApp photos of everything we eat to James, the nutritionist, and he studies the images, works out how many grams of protein, carbs and fats we've eaten, compares it to our training load and offers advice. Even by taking the photos, you become more aware of what you're eating and how much. It's hardest at home. What to buy? How to cook it? The solution comes from James, or Murph, as he's known: a food delivery service. He speaks to a local health food restaurant, and we get sent what we need that evening. Fanatical to some, sensible to us.

Less weight, to a certain point, means more speed, if you can keep your power up. Less weight means faster climbing for the same effort. Our bikes cost thousands of pounds in part because the frames are so light and the wheels so easy to rotate. We ourselves weigh six times what our bikes do. So if you spent months designing pedal cranks that are a few grams lighter than the previous ones, you will spend hungry weeks stripping any extraneous fat and unnecessary muscle from your own frame. What point is there in big biceps when the strength comes from the legs? Who needs pecs to ride a bike?

We are in a bizarre bubble where all normal is strange and all that is strange is normal. You jump on the scales in the morning, and if you have eaten slightly later the night before and not had your morning bowel movement, you'll be heavier than you thought you were. You'll look in the mirror and you'll think, yeah, I do look bigger, this isn't good. The very next day, after the usual trip to the bathroom, you're back down to the weird normal where you think you should be. 'Yep, I'm looking lean now . . .'

That's how your mind works on the eve of the greatest bike race of them all. It can be your best friend and your worst. Talk will go round the teams. Have you seen so-and-so? He's super lean. He's flying.

It's the hardest thing of all for me. Inside my slender torso there's a fat kid from Cardiff trying to get out. If I had stuck to the one-day Classics or the track, I could be bigger. It's power rather than pure weight that dictates your fortunes. To tilt at the general classification, the yellow jersey at the Tour or the pink at the Giro, means obsession.

I can go out and train and do six hours with hundreds of efforts because I enjoy it. That's the masochistic side of me. The weight thing is a much harder battle for me. It's every hour of every day. My body, naturally, wants to be seventy-two or seventy-three kilograms. I'm six feet tall. That would still make me unusually lean. For the Tour I have dropped to sixty-eight kilograms. That's getting on for a stone below what I'd naturally be, and I can only do it by committing totally. I've been lighter still, sixty-seven kilograms before the Tour de Suisse in 2016, but I was too light then, empty and powerless. It's an incredibly hard balance, and it was tough to accept when I had it wrong, but I needed to go through that and learn from it to get to where I am now.

There is no happy medium for me. I'm all or nothing. If I have one little bit of sugar, one small cake, I just want more and more. If I'm offered a drink I can't just have one pint. I'll want five or six.

It fragments your year into eating periods. In October, everything is about nothing to do with the bike. All that has been cut out all year, from food and drink to socialising, is crammed in. November is more of a 50/50 split between bike times and wild times and December ramps up to 80/20, the 20% pretty much being Christmas week in Cardiff. January until the end of July: all about salad and quinoa. I know I have the Tour, so I have the commitment to stop. Next to no chocolate, or pudding, or alcohol, the big treat a meal out with Sa before I head to a race or training camp. Even on those precious nights it's all about making the right choices. Go for the seabass over the burger. Steal a slice of Sa's pizza rather than have a whole one to myself. Have the soup to start rather than the tiramisu to finish.

British Cycling's psychiatrist guru Steve Peters used to say that motivation can come and go but if you're committed you can do it. My birthday is in late May, generally falling during a training camp in Tenerife. I might have a gin and slimline tonic, fifty calories a glass. I might not. It's strange, but when you're on it, especially at a camp, you don't even want it. Fifty calories adds up to nothing but it might all count one day.

With the Tour upon you, six months of monastic self-denial at your back, it's the hardest not to crack. Sometimes it all feels worth it. 'I'm feeling good, I'm light, I'm where I need to be.' Once the race begins, if you're feeling good on the bike then it's easier to stay locked on the diet. If it starts going wrong, your mind slips with it. You have one square of chocolate and suddenly you have the taste for sugar again. It's like when alcoholics say that they can be sober for a year, have one drink and be back to square one. I can understand the sensation, even though our obsessions are self-imposed and we can maintain them and also our health. To avoid rediscovering the yearning for sweetness, the team will remove all snares and traps in your way. There will be dried fruit and natural yoghurt. That's it. And it helps, even if at the time you're annoyed, you're, 'Why are you taking the options away? We're grown men, we can make a decision . . .' But as soon as it's not there, you don't miss it.

Even our own weird normal is no longer normal in the last few days before we race. It's peculiar feeling super-fresh, because the mileage and intensity in training has dropped right back. You know it's the right sensation to have but it still nags at you, because your routine is feeling so exhausted that even watching television from the hotel bed you are lying on can feel a bit too much. I have the need to have a little sweat every day just to feel a bit better in myself. When you're training, the amount and types of carbs you eat are based on what you've done and have to come the next day. Before long steady-riding days, carbs are kept to a minimum; before big efforts days we treat ourselves to a bowl of pasta. But you always feel like you could eat a little more.

In training it's about fibrous foods that will fill you up but are low in calories. Racing is all about simple, easily digestible energy. Fewer salads, less veg, more rice, more pasta. A couple of days before you begin three weeks and twenty-one stages of racing, you want to be fuelled. Now you're eating pasta, you start feeling a little heavier. You stand on those scales and see it confirmed.

The fixation can kick in again. Maybe I should cut back a little bit on the next few meals. I'm too heavy now. How can I do what I want to do when I've put on a kilo since last weekend?

If you don't know your body, if you don't have confidence in what you're doing, it's easy to crumble, to crack. It has happened to me in the past. Now I understand these thoughts are natural for me. I don't fight them. I let them float to the surface, notice them, let them drift away. What have I eaten? Okay, I've eaten this, this and this. There's no way I'd put on a kilo eating that, it's just fluid retention. It has been a wonderful change of mindset for me. Now I know what to expect and how to deal with it.

The game is a mental one as much as it is physical. You shouldn't stop weighing yourself, because then the void is filled by doubt and demons. Weigh yourself after training sometimes too, so you can see if you're hydrated, so you can learn that there are natural fluctuations that your body will go through. It's not just about riding a bike and producing good numbers. Be ready mentally. Understand your body. Learn to be strong and learn to love the weirdness.

The route of the Tour is announced the previous autumn. You pay scant notice to it because the menu is always different and always the same: flat days for sprinters, rolling ones for the breakaways, high mountains for the climbers and general classification (GC) contenders. There will be heat, rain, wind and pain. Then you arrive and little towns you have never heard of or climbs that featured years ago suddenly become critical to your hopes and dreams.

Noirmoutier-en-L'Île, Fontenay-le-Comte, and the 201km that linked them together on Saturday, 7 July. The route would take us across the high road bridge from the holiday island, rather than the Passage du Gois, the exposed strip of road that gets covered by the Atlantic Ocean at high tide and that caused chaos at the 1999 Tour when its slippery surface sent riders tumbling and organisers panicking. Down the coast, through those seaside towns, maybe with a stiff sea breeze triggering panic and breaks in the peloton, cutting east inland at La Tranche-sur-Mer.

I wasn't thinking about Paris in three weeks' time. I wasn't thinking about a win, or a podium, or even a top five finish. It was the journey rather than the destination. Stay in the best shape possible. Do everything right – position myself away from danger, keep the concentration in those little lulls where it can abruptly all go wrong, drink at the right times and eat when and what I should. If everything went perfectly, the podium seemed a possibility. But as soon as the notion would swim into my head I would send it flying away again. Control what you can control. Let the rest happen as it will.

I was certain my form was good. At the Critérium du Dauphiné, the week-long stage race in the hills and mountains of south-east France in early June, I had taken the overall win and I had felt in control. When I won Paris–Nice in 2016 it had gone down to the wire, my eventual winning margin across the week just four seconds, a frantic descent of the Col d'Èze to hold off the challenge of Alberto Contador. At the Dauphiné I crashed in the prologue in soggy Valence but got back on my bike and only lost a handful of seconds, and when we got to the mountains – against Dan Martin, and Romain Bardet, and Adam Yates, all great climbers, all men I would be racing against at the Tour – I gained time on some stages and was able to follow every attack on the others. It was almost comfortable, if riding at your limits in the high Alps can ever be comfortable. On the long final ascent to La Rosière I held off all those men. La Rosière would bring the first summit finish at the Tour, on stage 11. Confidence fizzed through me. At thirty-two years old, I was still improving.

After the Dauphiné we had stayed in the south of France to reconnoitre more of the Tour's big stages. In our last training camp I was hitting the target performance numbers on each day, sometimes exceeding them. Some critics were saying that these week-long victories meant little, that I would always crack in the third week of a Grand Tour because that's what had happened at the Tour in 2015 and 2016. Did nobody realise that I was riding in the services of Froomey on both of these occasions? There was no holding back for tomorrow, no conserving energy for climbs later in the week. I just happened to be high up on the GC when I eventually had a bad day. On one of those camps, Tim Kerrison had said to me, 'You know, along with Chris you're the only guy who can take this workload. All the other guys in the team need to do a little less on some days, but you are the only two who can take it.' That gave me heaps of confidence as well. So, I can back up every day in training with Froomey. As long as I don't do too much or do anything stupid in the race, I should be able to do it in France as well.

All the talk now, out on the Vendée, was of Chris. Over the previous weekend, the French media had carried reports that he would be excluded from the race by tour organisers ASO. Back in September he had returned an adverse analytical finding for salbutamol, a legal anti-asthma drug that he was using to manage his chronic condition. Although the process was supposed to be confidential, it had been leaked to *Le Monde* in December. When the UCI, cycling's global governing body, announced on the Monday of race week that the case was being closed, it should have been a total vindication. No case to answer. However, not all in the French media appeared happy to accept that decision, and the cynicism overflowed into some of the nation's more easily riled citizens. At the team presentation, there were boos from a section of the crowd when we Sky riders rode onto the platform.

Chris was coming into the race on a sensational run of big victories. The last three Tours, the 2017 Vuelta a España, the 2018 Giro. It was unusual for a star rider to attempt both the Giro and Tour in the same year, because it was felt doing the first left you compromised for the second. The plan at the end of 2017 had been that I would be given another shot at the Giro. The Tour would be Chris's. I would ride for him there if I still had the legs.

Then it all changed. In 2018 there would be six weeks between the finish of the race in Rome and the start of the Tour on the Vendée, rather than the established five, so the football World Cup would not clash with the Alpine stages. The Giro was the only Grand Tour Chris had never won. The organisers made it worth his while.

The message came down from team management. The Giro is for Chris. You can ride for him, or you can go to the Tour and race there.

I understood Froomey's motivation. I got that he was the dominant stage racer of our generation. I also couldn't pretend I wasn't disappointed. It felt like unfinished business to me; I was super motivated to go back and try to make amends for what had happened in 2017. Why has he got to do that?

Control what you can, not what you can't. I responded, 'I don't want to go for the Giro and ride solely for him. I'm going to get in the best shape possible for the Tour; you never know how Chris is going to feel after the Giro. I'd rather be the faster guy in the Tour than in the Giro. That's the plan, there's the motivation, that's what I'm going to do. Just go full out for the Tour, that's the best chance I've got.'

The compensation from management was that I would be a protected rider in the first part of the Tour. That should mean I wouldn't have to work for Chris. When I discussed it with other people, however, it became clear that protection meant different things to different people. Was there actually any substance to this strategy, or was it just a sop?

I rang up Dave Brailsford a few weeks before we flew in to the Vendée. I needed to be clear in my own mind. I had my idea of what I was going to be; I just wanted to make sure the team was on the same wavelength. Dave's answer was brisk: if you're feeling good one day and you're going up a mountain and Froomey gets dropped, you don't have to wait for him, unless you've already lost two or three minutes in the overall standings. I then had the same conversation with Nico Portal, our sport director, who controls race tactics mid-stage from the team car. His answer was subtly different but good enough too: Froomey is the team leader, and the boys are looking after him, but you are free to ride as you like around that.

Now I'm quite comfortable riding on my own in the bunch. Having ridden the madness of the track, survived the intense drama of the Classics, I can float around a group quite happily, choosing different wheels to follow, other riders to work off. The plan, when you put those disparate interpretations together, had a central theme: get to the second week and the Alps in the best shape possible, and then the roads will decide. There is no bluffing your form on those monstrous climbs. The stronger man will get the support of the weaker. It will be survival of the fittest.

Froomey and I only talked directly about it for a few minutes. He was positive about the plan. 'There's no reason why you can't be on the podium as well if all the boys in the team do their job. If you have to ride for me, G, then it would only be at the death, right towards the top of the toughest climbs, and at that point the group left at the front should be small anyway and you should still be able to keep going to the line.'

To me, he was pretty happy about me getting my own result as well. Just as importantly, everyone was clear as to how we were going to race it. We were less certain of how his form would be after the privations of the Giro, which he had won in such spectacular fashion on the final Friday. Froomey is always confident. He always says he's good. He always feels he can get the result he wants. At the same time, I could sense that he was not at his absolute best, the same form in which he had won four of the past Tours. He had struggled a little getting down to his race weight; the burden of the salbutamol case must have eventually had a mental effect. I still believed he could win, I just didn't think he was quite at the exalted level he had been in the past.

And I wasn't worried – not about the balance of power within the team, not about the way a few rogue Frenchmen might misinterpret the UCI's decision. I just wanted the Tour to start. You have trained so hard and for so long. Every time you climb on your bike in that final week you are analysing how your legs feel. Every pedal-stroke is data for your subconscious to obsess over. Before I had left the UK for France, I had won the national time-trial championships on the Thursday. On Friday, at home in Cardiff, I had done a short ride and felt a little stiffness in a joint in my back. I started to worry, even as I knew deep down I had nothing to worry about. The Tour amplifies everything – the hype, the reaction, the signals the body is sending to your brain. It's like Ed Clancy used to say: 'We've done all the work now, boys, the only thing we can do is fuck it up.' Two hours after he'd said this for the first time I was lying on the hard shoulder of an Australian road, bleeding internally, my spleen ruptured.

I spoke to our team physio Nathan, another Cardiff resident, about the joint stiffness. He massaged it, worked on the tightness, gave me some stretches to do. 'Keep working at it, you'll be fine once you get out there; you're just overthinking things.' He was right. It was a little tight; he was good; I would be fine.

Just get going. Before I left on Tuesday, flying out from Cardiff in the evening, Sara and I went for a coffee. Decaf for me, because I cut out all caffeine in the final few weeks before a Tour, even though an espresso is a rider's morning ritual and their treat halfway through a long ride. Go cold turkey and you feel the real kick when you need it in the last hour of an important mountain stage. Sa also had a cake. I had nothing else, proper regime. She looked at me in the café.

'I'm sad you're leaving, but I'm glad you're going now because you're turning all quiet. You're thinking about the race. That's all you can think about.'

That night, the country in the grip of a heatwave, I woke up in a pool of sweat. No fan in the bedroom, no cool air coming in the window. I went downstairs and went to sleep on the rug in the front room, where it was cooler than our sweatbox of a bedroom. Sara came down early in the morning, spooked by my absence. 'What the hell are you doing down here?' We both knew I needed Saturday to come round. My body had been built to race. Once I was in the rhythm of the race, the strange routine that was my normal, my happy would come back.

Wednesday in France. Three laps around the team time-trial course with the boys that afternoon, our pre-race press conference to follow. Every question was aimed at Dave and Chris. Most were about salbutamol.

Thursday a training ride, a little rain for the first time in what felt like weeks. A café stop for coffee or a sparkling water, and a World Cup sweepstake, instigated by me and organised by Luke Rowe, our road captain. Eight riders in our team, eight teams left at the quarter-final stage. Luke pulled out France. We shouted about a fix. England for Egan Bernal, whose native Colombia they had just beaten, Croatia for Wout Poels, Sweden for me. I tweeted a photo of the sweepstake standings and the message 'Come on Sweden!' Instant abuse from some Englishmen and women for a perceived lack of support. I actually wanted England to do well. That's social media for you.

Your hotels at the Tour are booked by the race organisers and handed out to the teams. The standard varies but so does the pecking order; a lesser place one evening might mean a better one a few stages down the line. We began well: most of us with our own rooms, all of us with air conditioning, which as the fierce heat burned away became essential. Sometimes sharing a room can be good – someone to talk to, someone with whom to have a relaxing moan. But the night before three weeks of the hardest bike race in the world, you want to be on your own. Torture for an elite cyclist sixteen hours before the Tour starts is hearing his roommate sleeping soundly when he himself is too twitchy with nerves to drop off. Then the talk is short and sour. 'You bastard . . .'

Saturday morning. The heat was already rising as we ate breakfast, all of us lean, all of us wishing away the next few hours. There is always so much collective anxiety in the peloton in the opening few days of the Tour, and as the 176 riders rolled out of Noirmoutier-en-l'Île just after eleven o'clock, you could feel the nervousness thick in the air. Big names have won opening stages on the Vendée: Miguel

Induráin in 1993, Tom Boonen in 2005, Philippe Gilbert in 2011. As always, a doomed break went away, one rider from each of three wildcard teams in the race – Yoann Offredo of Belgian team Wanty-Groupe Gobert, Kévin Ledanois of Fortuneo-Samsic, Jérôme Cousin of the local heroes Direct Énergie. Doomed because this was a day marked for the sprinters, and all the big guns were ready to fire.

Down the Atlantic coastline, while the television director showcased the beaches, we riders ticked off the day's Holy Trinity: Saint-Jean-de-Monts, Saint-Gilles-Croix-de-Vie, Talmont-Saint-Hilaire. All under control as we turned inland and into the Marais Poitevin, all marsh and farmland and green canals, the break being allowed out to four minutes before the sprinters' teams started to work at the front and bring them back in.

It was almost sensible, even when American Lawson Craddock stacked it in a feed zone and went down hard on his arm and head. But it would be a stage like the Dairy Milk advert featuring a gorilla drumming to Phil Collins' 'In The Air Tonight'. Tension building. Tension building. And then, with one clattering explosion, the madness descends.

We'd been riding second team in the peloton in relative calm. Relatively for the first stage of the Tour. In any other I'd have graded it super stressful, but the parameters change at the Tour. We were fighting to stay at the front, against other GC line-ups and the sprinters' teams. Inevitably the sprinters' lieutenants were moaning about the GC teams getting in their way, threatening to return the favour once we got to the Alps. Standard Tour bitching.

Then our team's first casualty. Egan Bernal down, right behind me. A Katusha guy almost had me in the curb too; I managed to stay up but Egan took more of a flick and ended up on the deck. It may have been Marcel Kittel. You don't hang around to launch an investigation and question witnesses, you just race on and thank a few lucky stars that you wriggled free while thinking, oh shit, Egan's down, but it's okay, he's not riding GC anyway. As long as he's physically okay then that's fine.

Then around ten kilometres to go, one great crash, halfway down the peloton. Richie Porte was caught up in it, Adam Yates as well. Arnaud Démare, the big French sprint hope, was delayed too.

At the front of the group, holding tight as the pace wound up, you allowed yourself a little sigh of relief. Maybe they are the *chute* for the day.

Instead it was only the first wave breaking. Just outside five kilometres to go, and this time it was Froomey. Riders massed along the road and one of the Katusha riders, maybe Rick Zabel, was suddenly out of room and swerving right; Chris was flicked sideways, onto the thick verge, sent somersaulting over his handlebars and into a field.

It could have been worse. The landing was on grass and soft; another foot to the left, and it would have been a bollard breaking more than his fall. Apparently there were cheers heard from some of those watching on big screens at the finish line. We would get used to that, and more. It was worse for others; Nairo Quintana, another of the big challengers for the yellow jersey, winner at both the Giro and the Vuelta, twice second at the Tour, avoided those first two pile-ups and then smashed into a traffic island with 3.5km to go.

I had no idea at first what had happened. I was further up the bunch, surfing the surges, trying to keep my own head above water. When word came over the team radio, I almost paused. There was a time when it would have been me going back to help bring our leader through to the finish. This time it was a job for others. I could keep racing.

You don't want to be drawn into the harum-scarum melee of a bunch sprint finish, but you have to stay close in its wake. The further back you slip, the choppier the wash. And so when I crossed the line in Fontenay-le-Comte in fourteenth place, close enough to see the blue jersey of Quick-Step's Colombian superstar Fernando Gaviria raising his arm in triumph for his first ever Tour stage win, I was flooded with relief. Around me were several other of the GC contenders – Romain Bardet, Tom Dumoulin, Mikel Landa, Vincenzo Nibali and Rigoberto Urán. All of us safe, when others were not. Froome came in fifty-one seconds back, a dirty graze on his right shoulder, Porte and Yates alongside him. Quintana was another twenty-four seconds further back still.

Had you told me then that fourteenth was the lowest position I would hold in the entire three weeks, I would have laughed at you. Laughed at you and tried not to get too excited. On the bus driving back to our hotel there was mainly a sense of contented weariness, of consolation that it had only been fifty-one seconds for Froomey, rather than a fracture or dislocation, that he was not behind Porte, Yates and Quintana at all.

There were also some mixed emotions for me as I watched the England v Sweden World Cup quarter-final on my phone. If Sweden won the tournament I stood to pick up a sweet 400 euros in the sweepstake. Equally I wanted England to do well, even with the total absence of Arsenal players. Egan was with England, because of the sweepstake, and Dave was too, not least as he had spent considerable time consulting with the FA and had shared several phone calls with Gareth Southgate. To have something to take your mind off the Tour was cool, particularly in the stress of that first week. Watching another set of sportsmen deal with the pressure and tension was surprisingly relaxing.

All of us, football fans or not, were glad to be underway, daunted by what lay ahead but pleased we were at last heading in its direction. Even after eight starts at the Tour, the old sway it held over me as a kid growing up in Cardiff was still strong. No one else at my school had even cared about cycling. It was all football and rugby. My best mate was a Manchester United fan, which was why I ended up supporting Arsenal; we could argue about fighting for the Premier League. I was the weird one who was into cycling. I was the weird one who shaved my legs, although I somehow managed to keep this from the boys at school by wearing trousers and tracksuit bottoms for PE. The first shave came when I was at the kids' Tour of Berlin as a fourteen-year-old and been persuaded by all the other lads there that it was the thing to do. I made a terrible job of it, rushing it in a Portaloo, emerging with patches of hair and dribbles of blood interspersed down my calves.

The Tour grabbed for me hard in 1997. Eleven years old, racing the Manchester Youth Tour, only three days long but on at the same time as the Tour. I won the first stage, and with it a yellow jersey. Wow, I thought. This must be what it is like ...

Jan Ullrich would win that year. I was drawn to him as the underdog, the young kid who appeared to have it all ahead of him. I got home from Manchester and tried to convince my dad that he should get the Sky television package so we could get Eurosport as part of the bundle. Sitting in my pyjamas in the family lounge in Birchgrove, watching the highlights when Giuseppe Guerini won on l'Alpe d'Huez in 1999, a spectator running out into his path to take a photo and somehow managing to knock him off, the Italian remounting and riding away to hold on from Pavel Tonkov.

The sun always seemed to shine at the Tour. The colours on television were always so bright. It seemed so far away from my world, a place of muddy football pitches in Heath Park and wet summers and Chinese takeaways on a Saturday tea time.

Even now, when I hear the voices of the old Channel Four commentators, Phil Liggett and Paul Sherwen, I'm transported back to that lounge carpet. I hear the theme tune, written by Pete Shelley of the Buzzcocks, all keyboard washes and descending melodies, and I'm a kid again, dreaming of that distant race. And now I'm here, and I'm riding, and the race is ready to unfurl in front of me.

Chapter Three

Chinese Burn

The Tour is a happy place when you're watching from home as a schoolkid. The race closing in on Paris at the start of the summer holidays. I liked Jan Ullrich and the kit he and his T-Mobile team wore, the pink jerseys with the three Adidas stripes and the black shorts; cycling shorts should always be black. I liked the Kelme team for their aggression in the mountains and the fact that they all seemed to be small climbers who could make the bigger men hurt. At the time I had no idea the dark deeds some were up to. It was all sunny days in a Welsh world that wasn't always the same.

There were so few Britons in the Tour that I didn't worry whether it was a realistic dream for me. I watched David Millar winning prologues and going into yellow, and I just knew that I wanted to do the same. Or at least try.

A leap on in years, and you find that the Tour is about stress rather than carefree fun. Sunday, 8 July and stage 2, another hot one in the far west of France, 182.5km in a jagged anti-clockwise loop from Mouilleron-Saint-Germain to La Roche-sur-Yon, a day for the sprinters again but another when all the big teams, whether they had a big man in their ranks or not, wanted to ride at the front. All were worried about crosswinds coming in off the Atlantic coast, because crosswinds splinter the peloton; there is no sense riding directly behind a rival when the winds come from the side, so instead thin diagonal echelons form across the road, and if you fail to get in one, you can find yourself disappearing backwards through the field at pace.

I'd actually have welcomed them. Echelons are dangerous only if you don't see them coming and aren't riding in the correct place with the right strength in your legs. When you're racing for the GC, you want days that are tough for you but more punishing for others. The smaller guys, the lightweight climbers like Nairo Quintana, Mikel Landa and Dan Martin – they're the ones who really don't enjoy winds or cobbles. Tom Dumoulin can handle them, Chris Froome can handle them. Vincenzo Nibali, Alejandro Valverde – these are the sort of grizzled veterans who can cope with almost anything. Adam Yates? He's a great rider, but you never know, he too could get caught out.

Instead, on a day as still as it was humid, you had competing trains of rival teams, almost drag-racing each other across the parched French countryside. Movistar on one part of the road, for Quintana, Landa and Valverde; AG2R for Romain Bardet. Quick-Step for Fernando Gaviria, Bora-Hansgrohe for Peter Sagan.

We tried to hold the left-hand side of the road. You think about where the wind might come from, and you instinctively seek shelter on the opposite side, but once we had marked our territory there it made sense to hold on to it. As always there were constant calculations to be made. You can sit in your own safe line but you then need teammates to ride in the wind for you, and if you do that you burn your collective matches at a much faster rate, at a point in the three weeks where you need to be conserving as much firepower for the big challenges to come as you can. You can try to hide in the wheels instead, but that adds that little bit more danger. I don't mind that so much, but Froomey prefers to have more space; let's just go on the side, boys, you boys can do it. I also didn't like riding directly behind Chris too often. The way he rides a bike obviously works for him, but it doesn't always fill me with confidence as a follower. Sometimes he looks down at his Garmin or his handlebars and maybe gets close to the wheel in front and twitches a bit. Which means if I'm sat behind him my heart can start thumping at a point when I want all to be calm, and I find myself wanting to be alongside or in front of him.

It's why we settled for the bubble shape rather than the long line in single file. Two riders at the front, Chris and I behind, two more to take over at the front when the first pair have done their turn. It kept us safer and it kept us from inadvertently dropping too far back. If you're the last in a line of eight riders you can have your leading rider in first place while you are back in fiftieth. The further back you are, the more likely you are to be caught up in crashes and splits. Bubbles rise to the top. Simple.

We also had the riders to make it work. Most of us had been riding together in multiple Grand Tours. Castro – Jonathan Castroviejo – has ridden for Movistar. He knows how it works. Egan was in his first Tour but is so talented he could soak it up immediately. He grew up mountain-biking, so he can handle his bike; he's aggressive in a good way, he gets stuck in. Even on this second stage, we could be honest with each other. 'Hey, Kwiato [Michał Kwiatkowski], stop coming past me. I know it's not deliberate, but don't overlap us.' You could feel it getting dialled in. We would look after ourselves.

A crash came towards the finale once again. This time it was Gaviria who was delayed, and Peter Sagan who out-kicked Arnaud Démare on the slight drag up to the finish to nick the yellow jersey. This time all of us came home safely, Chris included. Him a minute and seven seconds down on Sagan, along with Richie Porte and Adam Yates, me quietly up to sixth in the general classification, just fifteen seconds down.

Cliché alert: you don't win the Tour in the first week, but you can lose it. Bardet, Dumoulin, Landa, Nibali and Rigo-berto Urán were all nestled around me. So much of those first few days had been about fighting for position, and already the stronger riders were rising to the top. From the moment the flag had dropped to signal the end of the neutralised section at the beginning of each stage, the concentration had been total. Get to the front, battle to stay at the front. At some points, part of me had felt like saying, what are we doing? And the experienced rider in me would answer, you have to, otherwise you're going to be at the back. It's ride hard and fight or sit back and sink. You've got to spend energy to save energy.

A few days later I would find myself alongside the

Irishman Dan Martin during a neutralised roll-out. 'G! I've barely seen you yet. You boys are always at the front. What's happening?' You just had to shrug. Get yourself into the best position, worry about socialising when it's all over. Neither of the first two days was anywhere near as tough physically as the Alps, but the mental fatigue left me almost as tired. So calm on television, riders seemingly following their teammates without a hitch, so relentlessly stressful to ride.

It made the peloton an angry, noisy place. Each of the road captains trying to police it for their team, no one backing down, everyone up for it. Luke Rowe will never have too many friends outside Sky because he will get stuck in and do his job properly – refusing to take any shit, not caring in the least if he offends anyone. He never rode danger-ously, but he held his own, and he did what he had to do for Froomey and me. Imanol Erviti was doing the same for Movistar's trio of stars, as were Michael Schär and Stefan Kung for Richie Porte at BMC.

If you race well it is because you train well. And nowhere do I train better and harder than Mount Teide in Tenerife.

People think it's the altitude of Teide that sends us back there year after year as we prepare for the Tour. I don't think it is. I had three camps there in the first half of 2018, each of two weeks, and I didn't feel that was sustained enough to really benefit from sleeping halfway up a dormant volcano. It's the work you do there, the monastic lifestyle you lead. When you go to our training camp in Tenerife, you know you're in for a hard time, and you're also kind of excited in a masochistic way, because you know the end result is going to be good. The process will seldom be enjoyable and never be easy. But you know that if you do commit, the outcome will be worth it. Each year I had felt the power of that most Welsh-sounding of Gran Canarian mountains in my legs. The key to me feeling confident and calm coming into the Tour was knowing that I had done everything I could, and knowing that what I had done worked for me.

Monday, 9 July. Stage 3, the 35.5km team time-trial out and back from Cholet. It would be the first real test of that confidence and the form those camps should have created, although the fact I had been able to make my way up the peloton across the weekend and position myself as I wanted was an encouraging sign. The course was a difficult one, the parcours rolling and the weather blustery now as well as relentlessly hot.

I was being asked by journalists about the chances of me going into yellow. Sagan, brilliant all-round rider that he is, was focused on winning a record-equalling sixth green points jersey rather than the GC. We were known as one of the strongest time-trialling teams. So too were BMC, which meant Greg Van Avermaet, my nemesis in Rio, was eyeing that prize too.

You can't hide in a time-trial. When your legs are bad, as mine had been at the Worlds in Bergen ten months before, it's horrible. I was suffering at the start and I continued to suffer until the end. I was useless ballast to the team, a gasping sea-anchor. The guilt was almost worse. It's a team time trial, and I was doing nothing for the team.

That anxiety was tangible on the bus that morning. Everyone understood it was a big day; no one wanted to be the one who let his teammates down. Everyone getting ready at the same time, a large bus made to feel cramped by arms stretching into skin-suits and aero helmets being pulled on and adjusted. Luke was stressed. Time trialling is one of the weaker parts of his strong all-round game.

I tried to turn that tension into a positive thing. An atmosphere of expectation, of feeling alive as a racing cyclist. I'd had a couple of coffees to get the caffeine in, but I could feel my heart thumping for other reasons too. These are the days you train for and relish. You know that when you accelerate through the first corner all the nervous energy will dissipate, and the road will unfurl in front of you and the concentration will be total. As we rolled to the start and the commissaires came over to measure our bikes, as protocol demands, I could feel my hands tingling with anticipation. We sat as a team, focusing on the first kilometre ahead of us, and then the shout went up: 'Right, boys, two minutes, okay?'

Eight of us lined up alongside each other on the start ramp. Each man being held in place by an official, which works okay in an individual time trial, because the guy doing it is an expert, but when there are eight of you, inevitably someone gets the keen yet incompetent amateur. Sometimes you put out a hand to one side, which means please rotate me slightly that way, and they don't move. You twist around in your cleats and tell them you'd like to be moved. They panic and shift you much too far, and you stare silently out from behind your polished, reflective visor and think: oh man, I've got one of those ...

The beeps began to count down to our start. In the team pursuit on the track this was always my dark moment; the start was both critical and my least effective skill. On the road, almost ten times the distance ahead, there is less pressure, but the sound still fires you up. There is one with ten seconds to go. It's like being prodded. 'Phew, here we go ...'

A beep per second from five seconds out. I lifted my head, tensed in the saddle and took a big suck of air. Three. Two. One. Down the ramp, pushing hard, and away.

I tried to clear my mind of the doubts that were in there from the team meeting an hour or so before. Before every team time trial there is a collective conversation: what happens if so-and-so crashes or punctures? Do we wait as a team for them – either because they're the designated leader or because they can provide power at the front of the line – or do we save the time and cut them loose?

The call had been made and it came as a shock. We're only waiting for Froomey. Even though I was the backup leader, even though I was supposedly protected across this first week, if something happened to me, the boys weren't going to wait. This was different to what I'd talked to Nico Portal, our sports director, about the night before. We'd discussed waiting for the stronger riders up to ten kilometres to go. It seemed to make sense up to that point. The stronger riders' turns on the front, combined with more rest for the other guys in the wheels, would make up for the time lost having to wait for them.

Once Nico told me of the new plan before the team meeting, I made a similar point again.

'Look, G, we just need to have a discussion about it because we've been looking at it, and the rest of the team will probably lose about thirty seconds if you wait for someone.'

'Yeah, you might lose thirty seconds by waiting for me or Kwiato, but when we get back on, wouldn't you gain most of that back? You might get twenty seconds back and so end up only losing ten. By not waiting for me, by missing my turns at the front and the extra rest, you could lose fifteen to twenty seconds anyway . . .'

The thing is, there's no way of really knowing the answers to this. It's all conjecture – although saying that, the performance team probably have an algorithm on Dropbox that delivers all the answers. Management were obviously up all night having big talks about it and that was the call. I felt sympathy for them having to make that decision, and with Nico for having to deliver it. He knew how I would react. Luke stress-tested it too. 'Yeah, I get it, but won't we gain more by waiting up until a certain point for G?' 'Boys, we've thought about this. We've debated it. That's the call.'

I sat there and stewed. I'm an easy-going man but I knew what that meant. If I punctured and no one waited for me, I would be gone. I could lose three minutes. Any hope of winning the Tour would be gone in one hissing, heart-sinking moment. The chances of that happening were slim, but they certainly weren't impossible.

'Hmm. That's a bit shit, to be honest. Fucking hell, guys, could you really not wait for me?'

I couldn't let my mind wander out on the course. The thought wanted to creep in, through what our former psychiatrist Steve Peters used to call the chimp, and I had to block it off with logic. I'm not going to intentionally try to puncture or crash. What will be will be. Do what I always do and I will be alright.

I took the lead off the ramp as I was supposed to do. Through the first roundabout and I was locked in. No what ifs, just the road and the plan and the pain.

We all knew how long we were supposed to do on the front. Fifteen seconds a man as the basic rule. On this course, with its climbs and descents, we had to be flexible. Hit the front in a dip and you have to keep the momentum a little longer. When you're going fast, keep it short. When the road dragged, the stronger riders went a little longer. Luke would stick to ten seconds or something. Better that way, doing short turns and more of them, rather than him trying to do hero turns and getting dropped halfway through.

No time or need to communicate too much between ourselves, just Nico on the radio, reminding us what was coming up on the road. Our words were simple and designed not to confuse. 'Hold!' to keep the pace, to stop accelerating. 'Squeeze!' to step it up. Never 'go!' because 'go' can sound like 'no!' If one of us wanted to sit on, to take a brief tow at the back of the line, we made a thumbs down signal that

Nico, following behind in the team car, could spot straight away and call on the radio. 'Luke's sitting on now!' That way the next man knew to finish his turn and drop back in at seventh man, rather than at the very back, or else he would burn too much energy trying to then get into the gap left for him ahead of the struggling back marker. When Luke is ready to start pulling turns again, he waits for a full rotation, not a random amount of turns. He raises a hand so Nico can let us know he's back in. 'Luke's back in!'

We never changed just before a roundabout, because you don't want to be side by side with a teammate going round a bend. Too dangerous, too inefficient. Change early rather than late. When we came to a series of corners, the man on the front would lead through all of them and then get out fast. When it was Luke, we just had to bite the bullet.

Coming out of a corner, the discipline was equally as important. We didn't want to accelerate full gas straight away, because that would open up gaps in the line for those still in the corner, and gaps waste aerodynamics. A shout of 'Change!' if we wanted to come past the man in front, when we felt he was slowing more than the rest of us. When we did, the man whose turn was done would give a little glance to the side or under the saddle before he swung off; if the guy behind was overlapping, a crash was almost inevitable.

Egan was new to it. So new that it was actually the first time trial he'd done with the team and only the second or third ever. He was strong on the uphill drags if a passenger at other points, but that was okay. Each man in the team has strengths that are called upon at different times. His moment would come in the mountains. For now, he looked after himself. He did strong, short turns but didn't let his ego get in the way and try to do too much. Finish with the team, don't finish yourself. Afterwards he shook his head ruefully at Luke. 'How the hell do they ride so fast on the flat?' Talk about straight in the deep end.

When you're good at a time trial, when you're at the Tour and starting to realise that you're in really good shape, it just flows. It's almost like the faster you go, the easier it feels. But the pain is there all the time, a constant companion that you just try to cope with because you have before.

A five-hour stage hurts like a Chinese burn, if you ever experienced those in the playground. A time trial is more like a blister that has opened and keeps rubbing. More intense, on you faster. Paul Manning, my fellow team pursuit gold medallist from the 2008 Olympics, had a phrase that summed it up: 'Don't go looking for the pain, boys, it'll come.' Experience told me that I didn't need to be in the red on my first, second or third turn. Chasing it would mean I would blow long before the end. Watch the power numbers on the Garmin on my handlebars, work off them, trust in the calculations done by Tim Kerrison and the team.

It worked. BMC might have won the stage, but we finished only four seconds back on them. It meant Greg Van Avermaet did indeed take the yellow jersey off Sagan, who was dropped by his Bora teammates on the biggest climb, but I was up to third overall, only three seconds back. Our performance also helped Froome wipe out most of the disadvantage he had on the other big boys since that crash on stage 1. While he was back in eighteenth, fifty-five seconds down on Van Avermaet, Movistar could manage only tenth place, costing Mikel Landa and Alejandro Valverde almost all of the lead they had held over Froome and pushing Nairo Quintana even further back after his own crash on stage 1. Slower times for Romain Bardet's AG2R La Mondiale team and Vincenzo Nibali's Bahrain-Merida also saw Chris – as well as BMC's Richie Porte and Mitchelton-Scott's Adam Yates – drop back level with them.

I was strangely dissatisfied afterwards. I didn't feel like I'd got it all out on the day. I felt like I always hit the front on the fast downhill sections, so my turns were shorter than they might have been. 600 watts, but only for ten seconds, all of us flying. Rod Ellingworth kept me level as I warmed down on the rollers. Don't worry, G, save it for another day. We had a decent day.

Third in the GC? It was a great position for now, but we had seven mountain stages to come, and more than three-quarters of the race. The Tour hadn't really started yet. If I had gone into yellow, great. That I hadn't, I could cope with – though maybe if I hadn't been in yellow the year before, if I had never experienced it, if I hadn't been racing for the podium or more, if I had just been helping Froomey, it might have been different. I would have been more aggressive, in more of a rush.

Instead I felt unruffled. Don't spend too much energy, do the right things and let it happen itself if it's going to happen.

Don't go chasing it. It will come.

Chapter Four

Don't Lose the Wheel

Tuesday, 10 July. An overnight shift from the Vendée, north to the short steep climbs and hidden headlands of Brittany, a region in love with cycling the old-fashioned way, a place that has consistently produced riders to make France proud. Not least Bernard Hinault, five-time winner of the Tour, who had spent most of the build-up to this one taking repeated swipes at Sky and in particular Chris Froome. The headlines: Froome shouldn't be at the race; Sky ride in a way that betrays cycling's grand traditions. The subtext: if you boo them from the roadside, it certainly won't displease me; hang on, Froome's one win away from levelling up my record?

A start on the coast at La Baule, a long loop inland and then back out west to finish 195km later in the little town of Sarzeau. A little town just like many others, tucked into the inlets and wooded folds of Brittany, except for one thing: it was the home of David Lappartient, French president of the UCI, cycling's global governing body – and Lappartient and Dave Brailsford were having something of a public disagreement.

The French David had, like Hinault, been initially critical of Chris before his salbutamol case had been closed. The Welsh/Derbyshire Dave had told English newspapers at the weekend that Lappartient had the mentality of a 'local French mayor', and that to become more presidential, he had 'got some work to do'.

You could argue that he had a point, in that Lappartient actually was a local French mayor. But obviously Lappartient was then asked about it as we waited to leave La Baule. 'The last person who called me a "Breton mayor" didn't have much luck – it was Brian Cookson.' One sentence, two Britons taken care of; Cookson was the previous UCI president, who he had surprisingly beaten in an election the autumn before.

'By insulting me as mayor, Brailsford insults the 35,000 French mayors and the French in general. Doesn't he realise that it takes mayors taking stages of the Tour de France for such great events to take place? He doesn't understand much about cycling. When you are arrogant, sooner or later there will be always something that brings you back down to earth.'

That morning, I didn't have a clue about any of it. I was staying off social media for most of the Tour. I'm not naïve, but I had plenty of things to focus on. The white noise outside my little world just didn't impact.

Our press officer George tried to fill me in on the bus.

'Just so you know, don't get drawn into the Dave/Lappartient thing.'

'What do you mean?'

'Dave just said something this morning, that's the story at the moment.'

'I haven't seen him.'

'Even better then, just say that.'

'Okay, cool.'

That evening he would send me one of the newspaper stories about it. I messaged him back: I'm not going to read it, because then I can keep being honest when I'm asked by journalists and respond, 'I don't know what you're going on about'. The sprint stages are slow news days. There's not enough drama for everyone until the last ten kilometres. 'Let's ask Dave about Lappartient again.' 'Let's ask Lappartient about what Dave's just said . . .' At the Tour everyone there – riders, coaches, team directors, journalists, the blokes who drive the trucks, the performers who work the publicity caravan – are lost in the Tour bubble. It's part circus, part soap opera. Nothing in the real world matters. Everything at the Tour is magnified. At times like that, it is good to remind yourself that anyone who was not in La Baule or Sarzeau – or an anti-clockwise loop in between – really cared that much.

The booing on the roadside was certainly there. When you're whizzing past at 40mph you can't tell a 'booo!' from a 'Frooome!' As you were pedalling from team bus to sign on in the morning, you couldn't miss it.

You also couldn't quite work out what it all meant. One of our backroom team was manning an extra feed station out on the road when the bloke next to him started booing as a few of us flashed by. He asked the bloke why he was so angry. 'Oh, Sky shouldn't be here.' 'Why? What about this team, who have been banned for doping, or that rider, who has served a two-year ban for using EPO?' 'Oh, I don't know, I don't really follow cycling much. But Sky shouldn't be here. Definitely.'

It was pantomime as much as anything else. A few guys in the peloton from other teams told us how it worked: we would ride past a typical booer (average age: sixty-plus, usual pose: arms out, thumbs pointing down); once we passed, cheers would return and their thumbs would go skywards rather than Skywards. At least until deep into the mountains a week later when fluids started being thrown and a few rogue drunkards tried to grab us and pull us off. I was phlegmatic about it; I love France and I consider it a wonderful honour to ride the Tour. Almost all of the spectators roadside are fantastic. In the same way that I support Arsenal but don't agree with absolutely every Arsenal fan about absolutely everything, I was content that a few Frenchmen, at a race we all loved, had a few differences.

Some people appeared to find Sky's dominance irritating, or dull. It wasn't entirely logical to me; Quick-Step had cleaned up all spring but few were bemoaning their performances. Rugby supporters rightly laud the All Blacks for their peerless winning rate. Rafa Nadal is the constant king of Roland Garros, and Paris loves him.

France sometimes prefers its sporting geniuses to be glorious but romantically flawed. I thought of Richard Gasquet, the beauty of his one-handed backhand and his inability to win a crunch Grand Slam match against a less-aesthetically-pleasing but more consistent rival. I thought too of Warren Barguil, a Breton through and through, a talented climber but someone who admits that he prefers roller-blading to cycling, or Romain Bardet, dripping with talent but a consistent struggler in time trials. In 2014, the year Chris Froome withdrew with injuries after crashing and Sky failed to win a stage, we suddenly felt a lot more love from the locals. We were seen as flawed, but in a good way; more human, less predictable.

There was less rancour in the peloton itself. We had no sense of rivalry with Quick-Step, despite all their wins in the first half of the year. They weren't chasing the yellow jersey. We did with BMC and Sunweb, because they had Richie Porte and Tom Dumoulin, and certainly Movistar, seen by many as the strongest team. There would be discussion around the dinner table: those boys were burning a few matches today when they didn't need to, weren't they? Amongst individuals, I never felt it. I had a great chat with Greg Van Avermaet in the early part of the stage, despite him being in yellow and me being the man most likely to take it off him. We talked about the minutiae of football: which goalkeeper was the best in the world, the chances of Belgium and England in their World Cup semi-finals, the France v Rest of the World football match that *Vélo* magazine puts on every October. He's played in it a few times, I've never made it, and he was keen on a Wales/Belgium partnership in midfield. And so it continued. 'VAR, Geraint. What are your thoughts?'

You could compare cycling teams to their football

equivalents. Froome and I were there as the strikers, getting headlines for scoring the goals but entirely reliant on the creativity and defensive skills of those behind us. Gianni Moscon, defensive midfield. Kwiato, solid and reliable along-side him. Wout Poels the Mesut Özil, amazing when he's good but prone to the occasional off day. Luke sweeping behind the defence, Castro running all day down one flank, Egan Bernal the flamboyantly talented winger who will one day soon be given his own chance up front.

People would bang on about our budget, about the resources we could call upon. Had Greg pushed me on it, I would have argued that we were more Manchester City than Manchester United. We spent money but we didn't waste it. In the same way that Pep Guardiola splashed cash on Raheem Sterling and John Stones but improved them, Sky took Wout when Quick-Step didn't want him, a good rider then but a lot better now. Other riders have improved with the team: Chris, me, Kwiato. Luke, Chris and I all came through the ranks. It's not like we're going out and just buying Dom Pérignon. We've grown our own grapes too.

Critically, none of the barbs wounded us for the remainder of this stage. A four-man break of wildcard renegades – Dimitri Claeys, Anthony Perez, Guillaume van Keirsbulck and Jérôme Cousin – took the heat out of the day.

The sprinters' teams caught them in the final kilometre. Twelve, fourteen men back, sat behind the big men, seeing the empty road up to the finish line in front of us and Sagan going right and Alexander Kristoff going left. Right boys, just behave, don't do anything silly now. You pray that being that far back you have a little reaction time, knowing too that if they came down now, it's 50/50 that you'd go down too. You make your calculations and you follow a line of jerseys – maybe Fernando Gaviria's Quick-Step, since they know what they're doing and have a good sprint, or Dimension Data, because they're organised and you can sit on their tail, and they'll be owning one side of the road, which means if there is a crash you might have a get-out route, and they'll pick the right line round the corners, so that you're not going to shed places and have to burn matches trying to get that back. Follow the wheels, because if you don't and you hit the wind yourself, the watts will fly up and your finite resources, already stretched across the three weeks, will be frittered away before the mountains have even emerged on the horizon.

You try all that, but the sprinters' teams don't want you in there. GC riders mess up their plans. And so you respect that but not too much. You give the big boys space – Sagan, Greipel, Kittel, Cavendish. The next rung down you hold your position a bit more: Sonny Colbrelli, Bryan Coquard. It's not meant to be disrespectful, simply pure pragmatism. If you let every sprinter past you, then you're going to end up at the back. It requires flat-out concentration every second of the way home, or else you might find yourself like Froomey did in one sprint finish, fighting a guy in an unfamiliar white and blue jersey for a UAE wheel and getting screamed at. I said to him afterwards, 'You know that was UAE's Kristoff in the European champion's jersey, don't you?', and Chris looked suitably chastened. 'Ah. Right.'

The worst sprints are on big, main roads, dead straight, with headwind. Every man and his dog can get to the front, and then you hit the wind and everyone slows down and flaps from side to side. Horrible. While it's more stressful going into a narrow section because you've got to be in front to get through it, once you get there, it's a dream. It's a choice: do you want loads of stress and then easy, or a bit less stress but prolonged all the way to the finish?

The sprinters prevailed that Tuesday, as sprinters always do. Gaviria won his second stage in four days, out-kicking Peter Sagan and André Greipel on the final long drag. Greg, me, Froomey and the rest avoided a pile-up five kilometres out that left Katusha-Alpecin's Ilnur Zakarin stranded and Rigoberto Urán chasing frantically to regain contact. Greg would stay in yellow, his teammate Tejay van Garderen in second, me third those three seconds back.

No pressure, no spotlight. Wednesday's fifth stage would bring the hills for the first time all Tour, five categorised climbs over 204km from Lorient to Quimper. At the start, a little more drama that might have been avoided, us sitting on the bus and seeing a sixty-year-old man brandishing a 'Sky Go Home' placard. A comment or two: 'Couldn't he just come and enjoy the race?' Luke getting shouted at as he rode past, deciding on the spur of the moment to nick the sign as he went past, almost immediately realising that this could be turned into a bigger deal than it was meant to be. 'Oh no, what have I done now?'

You are glad, in moments like that, for men like Peter Sagan. Sagan is cycling rock and roll. He's the Zlatan

Ibrahimović of the peloton. He attracts attention, he relishes it and he plays on it. At his wedding, filming a recreation of the climactic scene from *Grease*, with him dressed as Travolta and his wife as Newton-John; pulling wheelies on mountain climbs at the Tour of California, eating cookies handed to him by whooping spectators.

With one stage win and two second places across the first four days, he was clearly in form again. As always he was loud in the peloton, impossible to miss even if the green jersey hadn't once again been glued to his back. Usually he is jovial and a study in relaxation, although a few days later he would have a huge mid-stage barney with Edvald Boasson Hagen, shouting at each other across four innocent and slightly amused riders, Mark Cavendish also getting involved from another five riders back, partly because Eddie is his teammate at Dimension Data and partly because Cav can never resist an argument. The angrier Cav became the more Sagan laughed, which had exactly the effect on Cav you might imagine.

The peloton respects Sagan. Everyone accepts that, along with Julian Alaphilippe, he's probably the best handler of a bike around. He can also wind riders up, because he's so confident in his skills that he can flick around from wheel to wheel. He acts like he's the only one in that space, which causes problems in a bunch sprint. For a sprinter he almost never crashes, and he was already the favourite for the green jersey, which would be his sixth, levelling up Erik Zabel's great record.

There's also a little jealousy, some fuelled by his success, some by the manner of it. Comments behind his back: 'Yeah, he doesn't even do his own social media ...' 'Oh, another wheelie ...' Another big win: 'The bastard ...' It's a touch tongue-in-cheek and it's also human nature. For me, there's never been any of that; we're totally different riders, we're never direct rivals. You can enjoy watching him at times simply because he's so impressive. I can think of two times when I just couldn't believe how strong he was. Stage 10 of the 2016 Tour, starting in Andorra, ending in Revel back across the French border, straight up the 22.6km climb of Port d'Envalira. Sky were riding our usual solid tempo, Mikel Nieve – aka Frosty, bearing in mind what his surname means in his native Spain – on the front, me on his wheel, constantly churning out 390 watts, 400, 410. Attacks kept coming, and Sagan appeared to be in every one. He's a sprinter. Sprinters are supposed to be too muscular and heavy for the steep stuff. I had felt okay keeping it steady, but I wouldn't have wanted to be jumping around as he was. Then, going over the summit, the break went away, and he was in that too and ended up second on the stage. The following day, a pure bunch sprint one, he was neck and neck with Cav. Bloody hell, I thought, he actually can do everything.

The second came later in the same Tour. It had been stressful all day, windy but not enough to split it. With around seven to eight kilometres to go, Sagan and Maciej Bodnar went clear, me and Froomey followed. It was like doing a motor-pacing session. I could only do five-second turns at the front before Sagan came through and kicked our heads in for a minute. Me and Froomey still talk about that day. And that was when Sagan had only won the first of his three back-to-back world road race titles.

The finish in Quimper was a draggy one. It had Sagan written all over it. Michael Matthews had failed to start the stage having been vomiting all night; Tiesj Benoot had abandoned after dislocating his shoulder in Tuesday's crash. Both would have been a threat, and their absence both eased the nerves – that's two men who won't be in the final mix – and added to it: look what happened to those lads, top riders, did nothing wrong but now they're gone. I had sympathy for them but was also glad I had escaped. In the same 2016 Tour where Sagan had amazed me, I had been caught behind a crash, somehow stayed up but got shunted into the barriers. I fractured a rib and told no one. What was the point? I could still ride. Back on the bike, back into another world of pain.

As a rider it is the casualties you notice and the traps that lie ahead rather than the beauty all around you. Those clichés of the Tour landscape – the field of golden sunflowers, the woman riding parallel to the race on a white pony, an old boy sitting astride an ancient bike while hanging off a crane, people running around in circles holding hands, making wheels for a giant bike visible to the television helicopter – all are invisible to us riders. Stage 5 may have had all of those. It certainly ran through the picturesque Aulne valley, and the cute film-set town of Locronan. None of that mattered. We cared about the percentage of the climbs, how the road narrowed off towards the finale through a technical section, how it twisted downhill and took in a steep right-hander before climbing again.

The panicked madness was afoot again in the final five kilometres. Somebody – I had no time to work out who – came under me in a corner and took me off Froomey's wheel. I drifted back to about eighth, ninth, tenth, telling myself it was fine, this was still okay, it wasn't about me for the stage win. Onto the drag, and Philippe Gilbert went away hard. Ripples from a move like that cascade back down the field. Shit, I should have fought a bit more for that wheel . . .

That afternoon coming into Quimper, heat coming up off the grey streets, I had nothing to gain and everything to lose. For a GC contender in a bunch sprint like the one unfurling in front of me, I was like a fly-half waiting off the side of a rolling maul, never involved in the brutal scrap a few yards away but still switched on, aware of everything all around me, ready for the forward breaking away or the prop bringing it all down. Holding my position, waiting for the sprinters' lead-out men to start peeling away, hoping they would get out to the side rather than coming backwards through an accelerating bunch like bollards in the road.

Sagan out the front, Colbrelli with him. Gilbert overhauled, Sagan taking it on the photo finish. If you excluded Monday's team time trial, Sagan now had two stage wins and two second places from the first five days. Rock and roll riding at its best.

Me? I came home in twelfth, close but not too close, fourth in the GC with Gilbert taking a few bonus seconds for his third place on the stage, Greg extending his lead to five seconds having picked up two bonus seconds earlier in the day.

The pack was lurking. Tom Dumoulin eight seconds back on me, Rigoberto thirty-two, Froomey fifty-two. All of us content to be in the scrap and with all guns still firing.

The abuse, the catcalls? Chris appeared to be dealing with it with his usual remarkable equanimity. As men we shared so much in common: eight years together at Team Sky, another couple before that at Barloworld. We lived in the same city, trained together, sat adjacent to each other on the team bus. We admired each other's talents and the willpower we had to deploy them. But whereas I was content to ignore social media and newspapers and websites, Chris reads everything. He's aware of what other riders say about him, what other teams are saying, what journalists are writing. The abuse he would either let wash over him or take it on the chin, using the aggression in the close-in battles on the tough days.

Once again his mental strength was proving his most impressive asset. I saw how much it took out of Brad Wiggins to win the Tour once. Once was enough for him too. Chris did what Brad did and then did it again, and again, and again. He then did it at the Vuelta, hit the training once again and snatched the Giro too, completing his Grand Tour hat-trick with the salbutamol case hanging over him all the while.

Training and racing would have helped take his mind off it. It would be the times he wasn't on his bike, the evenings, that I thought it must have taken a toll. It was his livelihood, his career, his reputation. Everything had hung on it. The most testing aspect was not being able to talk about it or offer an ongoing defence because it was a legal case. But it never made sense to me anyway. I know Chris, and I believe in him as a person. Salbutamol is not performance-enhancing; it's performance enabling. It shows up in every test, and as race leader he knew he would be dope-tested every single day.

While he had now been entirely vindicated, I wasn't sure if the hidden stress would have left him slightly short of where he had been in previous years. You can predict a great deal at the Tour. It is also an epic that defies control. Sometimes there are cracks invisible to the naked eye that only open up under the intense duress that the high mountains or third week brings. All of us were watching and waiting. We had been racing for five days but it still felt, to those of us hunting podium places, like an extended, hectic prologue.

I watched the England v Croatia World Cup semi-final that night on my phone in my room. That's the other thing about being five days into the Tour: everyone goes and lies on their beds after dinner rather than sitting around doing things together. Luke sent a message round the riders' WhatsApp group: if this goes to penalties, we'll all go to G's room to watch them.

There is an established way for a Welshman to watch an England team in action: when they win, you are British, when they lose, you are Welsh. Then there's Ben Jenkins, one of our soigneurs. He's English but lived in Wales for years, so his support just floats between the two, depending on who's winning. I would have been more than happy to see England go through, regardless of how the Arsenal fan inside might have felt about the number of Spurs players driving them on. I liked their panache, the obvious bond between them, the enjoyment they were taking from being on the biggest stage rather than being humiliated. There were lessons there for all of us watching.

Mind you, when Croatia prevailed, there was one reason to be relieved: Sunday would have been an England v France World Cup final. Imagine what that would have done to the reception on the roadside for a British team, especially if England won. First they win our race five times in six years, now they shatter the dreams of Les Bleus. What would Hinault and Lappartient have had to say about that?

Chapter Five

The Mûr

Thursday, 12 July. Sticky and hot, just like all the days that seemed to have come before. Stage 6, north from Brest to Lesneven, then south-east to Sizun and Carhaix-Plouguer and Rostrenen, but all of it just an extended hors d'oeuvres for two assaults on the beauty and the beast of Breton cycling culture, the Mûr-de-Bretagne.

If Brittany worships cycling, then the Mûr is the great cathedral. 2km in length, an average gradient of 6.9%, but in your mind far steeper than that, its first half rising up suddenly out of the narrow green lanes at more than 10%. They call it their Alpe d'Huez, except where the Alpe is all about the hairpins, the Mûr goes straight up in front of you like a take-off ramp.

Sometimes with climbs you only notice how steep they are when you come down them afterwards, back to where the team buses have parked at the base. You're too locked in to the effort of getting up them and the subplots and counter-attacks to take it all in on the ascent. With the Mûr you feel it both ways. And yet it's a good climb, one you can like rather than dread, because it's a slap to the face rather than a pummelling. Always incredible support on the lush verges on either side of the road, always the black and white stripes of the Breton flag. For a Welshman it almost feels comfortingly familiar. You see words of Breton that are almost exactly the same as their Welsh equivalent. A house is *tŷ* in Wales and *ti* in Brittany. *Bara* is bread and *hir* long in both languages. And while the Alps are vast, intimidating, foreign monsters to a kid from south Wales, Brittany and its coastline carry echoes of my own childhood. Short, steep climbs, twisting roads, hedges and oak and ash trees, little sandy bays and rocky headlands full of heather and windblown grass. It's Asterix and Obelix territory, plucky Gauls keeping the wider world at bay, *menhirs* on the hills, rebel spirits in the heart.

The Mûr is short and intense and oh so straight. You always think you can see the top because it's so steep at the bottom, but it's a false dawn – there's a crest and then it keeps going on, slowly dragging. Because it's short, everyone thinks they can get up it, climber or not. You can muscle it as well as fly up it.

To conquer the Mûr takes a real intense effort at the bottom. You know big attacks will come, and you don't want to be sprinting, but you have to accelerate and follow them. You fill up with lactic but it's still dragging and someone is still riding hard on the front, and that's how it bares its teeth. You can't pace the Mûr. You have to race it. In the Alps you might have twelve kilometres to climb up from a valley into the clouds. On the Mûr you have to go with its own rhythms and those of the riders trying to tame it. Like a berg in the Classics, it's about positioning. Get yourself to the head of the race, lead the charge in the top five, and it's your choice if you slip back a bit. If you're further back, you'll have to fight your way round someone if a move goes. Less control, more stress.

There are climbs that you enjoy, for the challenge they offer and the way they suit your special strengths. Then there are ones you just want to get done – and yet others you know you want to get done slightly less than the guy next to you, and so take a painful pleasure in it.

The Mûr, that Thursday morning, I wanted to get done. In such a short intense effort, positioning was key. Everyone knew it and so those final five kilometres or so before the bottom of the climb would be super stressful. For the stage win it was potentially a good day for a lot of riders, meaning more teams and more bodies to fend off on the run-in. It was good for pure climbers like Dan Martin, but also punchy musclemen like Peter Sagan. In a week's time we would have another climb from nowhere, up to the airfield at Mende, just as steep but half as long again, and that extra length would take it past the point where anyone could do it. On the big climbs of the Alps or Pyrenees, you have forty minutes to get to the front if you find yourself in the wrong position. On the Mûr it's five. If a gap opens up on a short brute you're going to have to put out some serious watts to close it up. You feel the Mûr not only in your legs but in the burn of your lungs. It's a prologue rather than a full stage.

And so the 100-odd miles to the first of the two ascents were like one long intake of breath before the explosions to come. A five-man break went up the road, New Zealander

Dion Smith at the head of it as he tried to steal the King of the Mountains jersey off Toms Skujiņš before the pure climbers would make it their own in the Alps. I chatted to Matt Hayman, years before a teammate at Sky, now at forty one of two riders in their fifth decade at the race. Matty had already told his wife to shoot him if he did another year of pro cycling, so that became the gentle tease to while away a few spare kilometres. Come on, mate, do one more lap with us. Either that or announce your retirement properly now, so we can give you a send-off and let you ride at the head of the race and take the plaudits as well as the wind for a little while.

It might sound like a counter-intuitive idea, but winning the Tour is all about the conservation of energy rather than its expenditure. You begin the three weeks with ammunition in hand but no more to pick up. Think of it as having twenty-one days to use one hundred bullets; they need to be used wisely. In the first week you cannot fire two a day, even if that sounds restrained, for you'll then get to the Alps when you might require ten each stage and find yourself running out in a far more important battle. By the time you get to the time trial in the third week, or the final mountain stage, you're completely out. Or put it another way, if you've ever been paintballing: don't be the guy who goes crazy in the first attack and sprays his entire magazine into the undergrowth in panic. This is a war of attrition. Stay in the game. Let others trail home early.

This was the big difference for me as I swung through those tight Breton roads towards the Mûr. In previous Tours my bullets were not my own to use. They were there to defend Chris Froome. No thought for hoarding or long-term plans, just repel all attacks on the leader. In 2015 I went hard for him from the start – riding into the wind, protecting him on the cobbles, never thinking about the next day, only that stage and everything I could do on it. By stage 19, I was close to the podium but almost out of ammo. I lost some time, knew I could use my last few bullets to limit those losses or let more drift away and save that remaining firepower for Chris on the last stage before Paris. It was a straightforward decision: we're here to win the Tour as a team. A year on, even after fracturing my rib, it was all about bodyguarding the general again. I gave him my bike when he crashed his. I got a stone in my wheel and had to change it, and when I did, I was offered no help to get back to the bunch. I lost bullets trying and I lost precious seconds again too. Only at the Giro in 2017 was I allowed my form purely for me, and the crash meant I didn't get to show any of it.

Be up at the front but not right on it. Stay out of trouble, don't lose time. Take a chance if you can, go for any bonus seconds you might grab without excess effort.

We would summit the Mûr once, take in a twisty descent round the back and then hit it again to the summit finish. The run-in to the first climb was super fast. No sharp left-hand turn onto its base as we had in previous races, instead a rapid straight drag through the village, across the main road and bang, into the climb at pace.

The organisers had hoped that double the Mûr would

bring double the drama. They should have considered the conservation rule. On that first ascent, everyone waited. Everyone saved their legs. Why spray bullets now when the real battle will begin on the second leg?

The descent felt long and twisty. With the lead group so large, we were dipping round the constant corners sometimes three abreast. Three men all leaning their bikes on a narrow road, all elbows out and fighting for the same optimum line, adds up to danger. A call round the team, an effort to get out into the clear air at the front, away from the crush and the crowds and the nerves clattering. These little micro-moves, so often overlooked in the greater GC picture, we were nailing again and again.

Control what you can. Risk only when the reward makes sense. When a moment came upon us where we needed to be at the front, everyone who had to be there – most of the time – was there.

There were two bonus seconds up for grabs a little further down the road. I was in a good position; I looked around and everyone was riding, chilling. Well, I'll have 'em then. It didn't take any effort – a couple of revolutions of the pedals, out the saddle, then looking back to see no one on my wheel and just rolling over the line. When is a Grand Tour ever won by two seconds? Even Greg LeMond's victory over Laurent Fignon in 1989 was eight seconds. But it was a little psychological nudge to everyone else, and more importantly meant I was at the front through the most technical section.

Kwiato, Egan and Froomey were with me, and when you're on the front, you can use the whole road. You can't conserve energy all day and hide too much; there comes a time when you have to use energy to save energy. Use your bullets to get in the best position for the battle to come.

If you're six places back and alongside two others, the option of where you ride is taken away. You're at the mercy of the other two riders. You see a right-hander coming up, you squeeze through that corner but then there's a left-hander, and now you're on the wrong side of the road, and you're trying to get past, coming, coming . . . and then you get squeezed out. Racing close to 60kph on a road just wide enough for two cars, twisting all of the time, is no longer fun. One mistake by anyone around – it doesn't have to be you – and it could be game over. You join in and battle for every position or you end up at the back before you know it. You can be forced to squeeze the brakes fractionally but this means you drop back a little. See the next right-hander and you start to move forward again but then there's another left. You're drifting around fifteenth and you're forced to brake for corners that those out front are sailing through. Using up bullets, and you're not even going uphill. Waste after waste.

Somewhere behind me, Tom Dumoulin was back in the wheels and got nudged by someone alongside him, and that little knock broke one of his spokes. An innocent little incident and suddenly he was stopped by the side of the road, waiting for a replacement wheel, the race accelerating away from him and back towards the Mûr. Panicked, desperate, he would then take shelter behind his team car and slipstream his way back up. Fifty seconds lost on the stage, twenty more taken away as a penalty for drafting. A rule but an unfair one; there's nothing to balance out the bad luck, and it's enforced only when the television directors show the chase in the first place. On the same day, another rider suffered similar misfortune, but French television coverage cut away as he got going again. It's either a rule or it isn't.

Onto the Mûr for the final charge. The first attack came from Richie Porte. I made an instant decision – okay, we've got to follow this. Adam Yates going next, all of us following, waiting for the next surge. All pushing hard, trying not to retreat into our own private worlds, to stay open to the moves and fakes all around. The lactic began in the legs and then, as I stood out of the saddle to get more power through them, started working into my shoulders and arms. I sat down, a moment's relief, and then back out of the saddle again, in and out all the time, never comfortable. A long climb like Alpe d'Huez is like that Chinese burn, a gradual ratcheting up of the pain until you want to yell out. The Mûr is a blister that appears fast and quickly turns bloody. From nothing to too much in a few tattered breaths.

It settled. This is solid, I thought, but I'm okay.

Dan Martin, in the white and black and red of UAE Team Emirates, launched down the left-hand side. I saw him go. I feel good. I could definitely go.

I went. A glance back under my arms to see if I was being followed. I was. Hold onto your bullets. Wind stiff on my face, making it harder still. Sod that, I'm not going deep here and helping everyone else.

I swung over, tucked in with my teammates again and

stayed there. Dan was up the road, gradually going away. Richie riding strongly on the front, I glanced down at my Garmin and saw that for the first time that day I was pushing out over 500 watts.

Jeez, Richie's going! 500m to go. Pierre Latour, the young talent from AG2R, jumped away down the right. Man, you're not going to go too far, we're all climbing too fast. Ah, you're strong. You will.

Win a stage and you take ten bonus seconds. Come second and you take six. For third it's only four. Maybe I could toss a couple of bullets on that.

Just as the sprint began to unwind, I saw Alejandro Valverde lining up. Another calculation in a fraction of a second: chances are I'm not going to beat him here, so just stay in the wheel and save it. Save it for when it really matters, up on the mountains ahead, in a sprint finish that will bring much more than this.

I crossed the line in ninth place, on the same time as Julian Alaphilippe, Adam Yates, Primož Roglič and Peter Sagan, Dan taking the stage win by a second from Latour and three from Valverde. Only briefly did I wonder what might have happened if I'd jumped a bit sooner. I knew that if I'd gone full on for that stage, if I went flat-out on the cobbles that would come on stage 9, I was just spraying bullets.

I'd seen it with Simon Yates in the Giro d'Italia two months before. Simon had ridden brilliantly over the first two weeks, picking up stage wins, jumping away from Froomey and Dumoulin, making punchy attacks and surges to build a solid lead with three days to go. And then he had blown, all the bullets gone, and dropped from *maglia rosa* to man overboard in one cruel afternoon.

I'd moved into second in the general classification without even trying, thanks to those two bonus seconds. Test batsmen don't score a century in a single shot. There are lots of ones and twos that you can't even recall at the end of the session. But they add up, and they tire the opposition, and they build your confidence. I had just nudged a single round the corner for one. Alastair Cook today, Chris Gayle on another.

Froomey? Froomey had maybe just survived a tight lbw shout. While Dumoulin was the big loser of the day, now a minute and twenty-three seconds back on the yellow jersey of Greg Van Avermaet, Chris had slipped five seconds back in the last kick on the Mûr. He was now fourteenth, almost a full minute behind me.

He had stuck with his usual tactic of pacing himself up the climb rather than spiking with the rest of us, lost a little ground and then found other riders getting dropped in front of him. I wondered if sometimes he could be too calculated: 'I shouldn't ride this fast at this point because I can't ride like this all the way . . .' It can be a great strength for him. Just like Dumoulin, he can grind all day, not worrying about this attack or that, comfortable in the knowledge he can ride it back. Yet on a climb like that, you don't have much time to ride it back. There are points in a race when you've just got to race and go with it.

I wasn't thinking of Chris as a rival. Test cricketers take confidence from their partner down the other end playing their shots, and it's the same in a Grand Tour team. If your leader is picking up time, if on every mountain stage you're both there at the sharp end, the whole team grows with that and the collective conviction snowballs. At least we could tell ourselves that it was less a matter of form with Froomey and more how he was trying to ride it.

I was still feeling good. It's not often you're able to decide how you're riding at the Tour. You're either full gas holding someone's wheel or you're sprinting for the win. I was able to make decisions and then implement them just as I wanted. No one was dictating to me. For once I was the master of my own destiny.

Confidence can leach away. You get a puncture, you have a little crash, then you seem to have another. The thought worms into your brain: bloody hell, it's going to be one of those years. But confidence can build, too, in the same subtle, incremental manner. A stage when I had made time on Dumoulin and Rigo and Bardet. Another stage riding in the right place at the right time from thinking about it and working it out. No crash, no puncture, no wobbles. Me riding as I wanted, legs good, bullets tucked away for another day and a greater fight to come.

Rod Ellingworth

Performance Manager at Team Sky, former head of British Cycling's Under-23s academy

I first saw Geraint on the track at the national championships when he was about fourteen or fifteen. A friend of mine who also worked for the British Cycling team, Tim Buckle, said, 'You need to watch this kid, there's something about him.'

Kids at that age are all on restricted gears to protect their legs. They're all pedalling pretty quick. But just the way he was carrying the pedals around, the way he sat on the bike – when you've been around the game for a long time, you see something. I was on one of the bankings watching him coming towards me on the straight, and he looked mint. I just knew. This kid is good.

I got to know him through his junior times. From then to now, his attitude never changed: really committed, really grounded, really honest. I soon realised that you don't have to motivate Geraint. You have to hold him back. When I used to write his training plan, if I wanted him to do four hours, I'd say do three and he'd do four.

When we first went to Italy with the British Cycling

academy programme, it was bloody hard. It's only bike racing, but in our little world, Geraint was a young kid and I was a coach thinking, I want to try to do my best for these lads, because they love riding. We didn't have a clue really what we were letting ourselves in for. The Italians didn't particularly like us. They used to shout over the race radio in real broken English, 'British, you fuck off!'

There was a moment where G was in a race, on his own between the front group and the peloton. Two cars went past him with a load of Italian lads holding on for a free tow, and they were shouting to rub it in – 'Inglese! Inglese!'

Geraint's reply was simple. 'I am not fucking English, I am Welsh, you twats!' He wasn't worried that there were ten guys hanging on, that he was losing position, that they were cheating. It was brutal racing, and he was tough enough to handle it, even as a young kid.

Chapter Six

Five Hours of Nothing, Forty Minutes of Everything

F riday, 13 July. Stage 7, across the great agricultural plains of northern France, from Fougères to Chartres.

These are strange days for us riders. 231km, the longest single stage of the three weeks, in some ways five hours of absolutely nothing happening followed by forty minutes of a lot happening that doesn't actually have any effect on those of us chasing the yellow jersey.

There is a decent consensus now in cycling that says these stages are too long. Cut it down to 160km and you'd still get the madness at the end as the sprinters' teams fought their turf wars. As I rolled past the politely applauding citizens of Fougères, glanced down at my Garmin and realised how many hours I would be pedalling for, with barely a bump or tight bend between me and the finish arch, the argument made a great deal of sense. In a weird way, too, I was quite content. There is something super-traditional about the long, flat stage in the first week of the Tour. We love this race for the avenue of fans parting for us on the fearsome climbs of the Alps, for the noise and beautiful chaos that the Basques bring to the roadside in the Pyrenees, for the finale riding multiple laps of the Arc de Triomphe and Place de la Concorde. The tedious transitional stage is just as much part of the rhythm of this long-form epic as any of those, a custom that goes back right to the race's inauguration, an elongated pause for breath in the middle of so much eyeballs-out racing.

On days like this you wait for the break to go away. It's doomed, of course; everyone knows that. It'll be caught whenever the peloton decides to catch it. But you all want it to go, because then everything can settle down and the usual well-worn plot comes into play. Unless, that is, one element changes: the wind.

200km in more or less the same direction all day. No real shelter out there, just the odd small village and kilometre after kilometre of open fields. Only a slight headwind this time, around 8kph; we Sky riders were warned about it in our team meeting. Had the wind been stronger and from a nastier direction, it could have been one of the hardest stages of the Tour. A nightmare for some, although I was kind of hoping that it might turn out to be crosswinds all day. I was feeling good and the team was riding well together. Make it into the front echelon on a day like that and you can quickly gain minutes on some of your big GC rivals.

These long stages may be traditional, but the way we race them now has changed their nature. Normally some of the smaller, second-division teams who might not have a sprinter will get a rider or two in the breakaway. It's an opportunity for their sponsors to soak up five hours of television exposure. Today no one wanted to, and so it turned into a bit of a joke. A few guys pretending to attack, then stopping on the side of the road. We were rolling along at 30kph, everyone just hoping someone would go, the more the better, ideally four or five riders. They could then roll through and off at a decent tempo and we'd all get to the final hour a bit quicker. That morning everyone knew they were doomed if they went, especially into a headwind. Too many bullets for too little reward.

In the end it was Frenchman Yoann Offredo who went hard and got away, all on his own, to make it both a great day and a horrible one for him. He would stay away until ninety kilometres to go, when his compatriot Laurent Pichon had a dart instead. Pichon would in turn be given fifty kilometres of his own until the peloton breezed onto his scent, sucked him back in and spat him out spent and in pieces, like corn from a threshing machine.

More accepted conventions followed. Ten minutes after the break went, we all stopped by the side of the road for a nature break. It is possible to do this on the move but it takes some practice. I'd say my success rate is 50/50. The more I need to go the easier it is. Froomey struggles, much to the annoyance of Luke, who is usually the guy who has to stop with him and bring him back to the front. Remounted, you wait to see which team will ride at the front and keep the break where we all want it. When there is no dominant sprinter it can lead to general bickering and indecisiveness. 'You guys go first.' 'No, you, we'll come later.' 'Can one of you please decide?' The team with the yellow jersey would normally take it up first, but this being BMC, with Richie in the team, they knew they had a lot of hard yards to come. Luckily for them, Fernando Gaviria was in such good form, and Quick-Step so dominant, that they were straight to the front. Tim Declercq, with his massive frame, broke the wind not only for the man behind him but for anyone within twenty feet.

We should have been able to relax. There was a slight headwind, meaning that even if we switched direction and crosswinds briefly split the peloton, it would surely all come back together as soon as the headwind reasserted itself. To give us the heads-up, we had Rod Ellingworth in the recon car around twenty to thirty minutes ahead of us. He would let Nico Portal know of any major changes of direction, what the wind was doing and if it could cause us any trouble. We were relaxed compared to other days, but you always have to be ready – top twenty, eyes and ears always switched on.

Sure enough we did change direction and the wind hit us from the side. We knew it was coming but didn't know how teams would react. AG2R hit it as a team and took it on, the rest of us all thinking, what, where are you going? We'll be in the headwind again in four kilometres with one hundred miles still to go . . .

This is the Tour. Expect anything and assume nothing. We all knew the move had a ninety-nine per cent chance of not working, but you'd still rather be in front than behind stressing. Not much chat amongst us all, because we were all now on edge, not wanting to drift back in case another futile attack came in. We knew, as we sailed through the little farming towns, that when we got strung out round corners it would take more acceleration out of them to stay in touch with the next man if you were fifty riders back than ten. Don't waste the bullets; try to recover some instead, *Call of Duty* style, by fuelling up right, eating and drinking in any relatively calmer interludes that you can find.

I was used to long rides, both in training and racing. I knew the little tricks to make time pass. 230km didn't sound that long any more. When I mentally converted it to miles, a habit that began when I was a junior racing on the Continent for the first time, it made it much worse. 143 was a smaller number but had a more deflating impact. Kilometres initially seem daunting but fly by more quickly. As a junior, 143 miles was unthinkable, especially on the seventh day in a row. 230km? Ah, that's not too bad. The equations you spin on the road.

As a kid, my first long rides had been about fifteen miles, out from Birchgrove to the lanes around Lisvane or Caerphilly mountain. As I got older I would venture out to the Storey Arms outdoor centre in the Brecon Beacons, thirty-odd miles there, past Merthyr and on into I had no clue where. The first time I did it was on a frozen winter morning, following the bigger lads from the club, absolutely no clue where I was, thinking to myself: I can't get dropped now, or I'll die out here, lost and alone. I remember telling Luke Rowe's dad about it the following day and being astonished that, as a cyclist, he knew exactly where I had been from the only two descriptive elements I could remember: 'Ah, I think we turned left over a bridge and out across a moor?'

The older guys had seemed so strong. They could ride for miles without a gasp. I would have to fuel up like a kid setting off for the South Pole – a big Chinese takeaway the night before, ham sandwiches wrapped up in foil and wedged in my back pocket on the ride, a full Sunday dinner waiting for me when I got back to my mum and dad's. There will never be a better feeling than piling into roast lamb, gallons of mint sauce and a heap of roast potatoes after sixty miles of south Wales' lumpiest roads.

I became obsessed with going longer each week, trying to better myself. Sixty miles one weekend, sixty-four the next, trying to get to seventy the Sunday after. I could feel myself getting stronger and fitter, more able to cope with the distance and the strain. Challenging myself, feeling good when I could handle it, loving the sense of exploring what felt like unchartered territory, even if every metre of it had been ridden by generations of Welsh club riders before me.

With no sign of the twin spires of Chartres' famous cathedral on the horizon, this stage had none of those rewards. Counter-intuitive though it may be, a six-hour ride in the mountains can feel less tiring than a long stretch like this on the flat. There is more mental stimulation in the hills, always something to break the monotony – a descent, a climb, a valley. On this stage there was only the feed zone one hundred kilometres in to look forward to.

This was at least the first day I could have a brief chat with other guys during the stage. I found myself next to Cav.

'G lad, you tried these new gels? Fruit salad flavour and vanilla.'

'Nah, we don't have them yet. Swap you two of them for a couple of speculoos-flavoured rice cakes?'

Everyone likes an easy day, but this was just too easy. More of those little tricks to fool the jaded mind. Scroll through to the map screen on your Garmin rather than the one showing time elapsed or distance left. Act like your mum when you were a kid on long journeys in the family car, giving yourself something to eat every half-hour. But you always have half an eye on how much you've done, and you're inadvertently calculating how far to go. Our team rice cakes are superb nutritionally but not quite the same treat as a packet of crisps or a lolly back then.

It was yet another hot, enervating day. So drink, and drink some more. You don't have to be attacking or sprinting to put stress on your body. Fail to fill the tanks when you can and you will crash when you least expect it.

An hour to go, and I was aching more badly than I would on Alpe d'Huez in six days' time. In the mountains you are out of the saddle and then back on it, moving around with the challenges of the terrain. On the flat you are seated almost all the way, and your backside tells you about it. It's like being on the stationary rollers for six hours. Your palms hurt from contact with the same part of the handlebars. Your wrists ache from being locked in an identical position for hour after hour.

Only with twenty kilometres left did the sleepy pace finally reawaken. And then we switched from riding easy to fighting for every inch of road, everyone conscious of being in the right place, the internal parking sensors going off in all our brains. There are always a few in the pack who are too cool to ride at the front. They like to cruise at the back of the bunch all outwardly relaxed. It's less cool when some bloke in front of you drops his water bottle and you go from chilled to sliding along the road on your shoulder and thigh.

Chartres at last, up ahead in the heat haze, the dark road cutting through fields of wheat stubble and green maize. We Team Sky boys stayed safe on the left-hand side of the road, Luke and Gianni Moscon and Castro working the tempo now. Wout had done his job for the previous 200km, never riding in the wind unnecessarily but the man holding us in position moving into the wind when he had to. Now he could relax a bit and drift back, thinking of the Alps to come, happy to stay clear of the frantic pace. The pace accelerated and quickened again as we hit the city streets, this time LottoNL-Jumbo's Dylan Groenewegen storming past Gaviria in a yellow-and-black-shirted blur to take his first stage win of the Tour, Peter Sagan close as ever in third. Van Avermaet had picked up three bonus seconds on the road but I was still in second and still to leave my bike unless voluntarily.

As on the Friday, so on the Saturday. 14 July, Bastille Day, few fireworks or fête on the 181km from Dreux to Amiens, Paris left untouched to our right as we swung north of the capital and headed for the far north-east and the cobbles to come on the Sunday. Because it was Bastille Day, we all thought the French would be gunning for the breakaway. Another tradition, a different plot to the day before.

It wasn't. Traditions stay and then change. No Frenchmen in the break, Groenewegen the strongest in the finish once again, holding off Gaviria and André Greipel this time. One more bonus second for Greg, but with the Alps two days away, a lead of seven seconds was as likely to last as snow on the south-facing slopes, whether it would be me who dethroned him or someone else.

I still wasn't worrying too much about my position relative to the other big boys. A minute can go in two kilometres of racing on the summit finishes. I had begun on the Vendée with a subconscious list of maybe ten guys, all of who could have been good. Richie, Dumoulin, Nibali, Bardet, Yates. All three of the Movistar guys. Primož Roglič and Steven Kruijswijk. Froomey. As the race goes on you get a sense of who's good and who's bad, and you almost find your place in the peloton by default. Still little of it carries much weight until you hit the mountains. If any of those contenders had a bad break, whether it was Richie getting caught behind that crash with Yates or Tom and his broken spoke, we wouldn't have gone to the front and worked to try to put more time into them. It's not the done thing. Don't try to capitalise on the misfortune of others. In the language of the peloton, don't be dicks.

It's the concentration that exhausts you. Those two days from west to east across the north weren't anywhere near as physically tough as what was to follow on the road to Roubaix and in the mountains, but the mental fatigue left me almost just as tired. Pretty much from the white flag being waved at the end of the neutralised roll-out to the finish line, the attentiveness had to be at one hundred per cent. I spotted Dan Martin before the flag had been dropped one morning. 'Hey G, I've barely seen you yet!'

Yep, and with good reason. Fifteen kilometres out from Amiens, Dan came down heavily in a crash halfway down the peloton. It came out of nowhere. He went down hard, lost a minute and sixteen seconds and dropped to thirty-first overall. Two days before he had been triumphant on the Mûr-de-Bretagne; now he was in so much pain as he crossed the line that he had to crawl up the steps of the UAE Team Emirates bus.

We took a little abuse on Twitter after that. We were at the front when Dan crashed, on the left, trying to stay out of trouble. The keyboard warriors saw this as us trying to gain more time on his bad luck. As usual they had misread it. We were so close to the finish the speed was there anyway. We weren't going to drift back into the peloton and risk something similar.

That was the one thing I wouldn't miss about that first week, the needless stress. When you're watching on television, it looks so calm. Guys following teammates, the ranks of their rivals obligingly parting. When you're in it, it's just bonkers. And that was the supposedly easy stuff.

Chapter Seven

The Cobbles
and the Cup

Sunday, 15 July. The day of the Fifa World Cup final, a day of reckoning in the Tour. Stage 9, from Arras to Roubaix, right up on the Belgian border, not long at 156.5km but all about the rough stuff in between.

There have been cobbles many times before in the Tour. We came across them in 2015, when I helped pilot Chris Froome between the gutter and the stars en route to his second yellow jersey. We hit them in 2014, when Froomey crashed on the way in, struggled through them and then withdrew as the pain from his injured wrist overwhelmed him. The great – and terminally stroppy – Bernard Hinault had punctured on the pavé in 1979 and lost almost three minutes.

No one in the peloton had ever raced over almost twenty-two kilometres of them in a Tour stage, spread across fifteen secteurs dotted in a long jagged line north from Cambrai and Marchiennes to Pont-a-Màrcq and Cysoing and then the town of Roubaix itself. We wouldn't be finishing in the famous old velodrome, the iconic crescendo of Paris–Roubaix each April; there wasn't the capacity to handle over 170 riders all clattering and elbows out. But it was the pavé that the thousands of spectators had come for, the pavé that the organisers hoped would provide a thriller for the millions watching at home from their sofas. They had even arranged the start time so that we would be done, faces smeared in dirt and sweat, just before the World Cup final kicked off.

You love or hate the cobbles for the same reason. Uneven, unpredictable, a bone-shaking demolition derby that favours the strong and the brave and the lucky and punishes the scared, cautious and skinny. These were not the smooth little bumps found in old market towns back home. They stuck up and they stopped tyres, closer to the shape of a melon or a baby's head. When they weren't there, it was even worse, because your front wheel disappeared into the hole. They aren't laid nicely side by side. It's as if a truck has driven down a field and some bloke has just thrown them off the back as he's gone along. When it was dry, the dust that covered them would rise up under the jackhammering of wheels and fill the air and your eyes and your throat. When it was wet, that dust became mud and turned an already slippery surface into treachery.

That was the cobbles. Because of the cobbles, every piece of tarmac that led into them would transform into a bunch sprint. The pavé is narrow. You can get a car down there but only just. When you're on your bike, there is one good line and there is sliding and bumps and punctures ahoy. You have to be up front, not only to pick that line but to avoid the crashes that inevitably follow all the bad stuff.

If the first eight stages had been stressful, this was going to be traumatic.

I like cobbles. I've always ridden well on them; I won the junior version of Paris–Roubaix as a kid. I loved riding the Tour of Flanders, which has cobbled climbs too, albeit a lot smoother than Roubaix. I had the build for it, taller and more muscled than the climbers, but that was before I'd slimmed down to compete with those same climbers in stage races rather than tilt at one-day Classics. I'd raced so much in Belgium as a kid that this landscape of flat, dark fields, of red-brick houses with shutters, grey roads and constant wind, slag-heaps and old mines and canals, felt reassuring rather than intimidating.

Breakfast, for the team, was a nervy affair. On the bus you could sense the tension, just as you could before the team time trial six days before. Everyone understood how big a day this was. For the climbers, Wout Poels and Egan Bernal, there was no expectation that they would be leading the team charge into the secteurs. For them it was about pure survival. Get thrown around, hate every minute of it if you have to, but get through it. A different sort of anxiety, but an apprehension all the same.

One of the biggest worries was the risk of punctures and crashes. Most of the time there's nothing we can do. Try to stay out of the gutters as much as possible, but not much else. This time we had a new solution: forty-five 'zone-hoppers' out on the route. These are guys, usually eight or so of them, who in the Classics drive between certain points on the route with spare wheels and fresh bottles. During the Tour stage they wouldn't be allowed; the crowds were expected to be too big. So we just had to get more and spread them out. Our second sport director, Servais Knaven, did well. Every secteur had guys at the end with bottles, with gels attached, plus spare wheels, and on most of them a man or two halfway along too, all in high-vis yellow. In the Classics the advice from the old-timers is straightforward: 'Just keep riding, even if you puncture, keep riding.' This time we had a better plan.

We talked about the team's tactics. Luke Rowe was excited, because he's a Classics rider, and so was Servais, who grew up on roads like this; he knew every twist and bump and crosswind. I was sucked into it all happily. I knew that less than a mile away on the BMC bus, Richie Porte would be dreading the day, that Nairo Quintana and Mikel Landa would have eaten the breakfast of condemned men at the Movistar hotel. We worked our way through the secteurs in the order we would meet them: right, boys, it's a sharp left into the first one, l'Escaudœuvres-Thun, just after we've left Cambrai, and that's 1,600m long, and then it's 10km on the D61 before we hit the next, d'Eswars à Paillencourt, and that's a long one too, and it's got a couple of tight right-handers along it where the crown of the road is super-steep so you want to drop into the nearside gutter for 40m or so . . .

All the early instructions were about being close to the front and safe, for these were only the appetisers. It would really kick off at secteur four, when they would come thick and fast. This is where the real damage could be done.

We were getting more and more pumped. Could we attack after this secteur? It's short but nasty, we could get quite a cheeky little break in if we went there. And Nico Portal just sat there looking quizzical, and then stood up and said, 'Boys, I know this stage is being talked up as a mini Paris–Roubaix, but it's not actually Paris–Roubaix, is it? If you try to get away there, is it really going to stick? You've got fifty kilometres to go, and how much time do you honestly think you can put into someone when they've got all that to chase back? We're treating this as a one-day race, when it's just one stage of twenty-one. Are you going to win the Tour here? No. There are too many contenders and too many well-oiled teams. You could lose it, for sure, if you went down, or got sucked into the dirty air behind the lead group, but this is less about winning the stage than not messing up the entire three weeks.'

He was absolutely right. At Paris–Roubaix, every rider wants to be there; every rider is built for it. But if they fall too far back to contest the win, or their job for the team is done, they could stop and it wouldn't matter. (Not that anyone wants to stop in Roubaix; it's arguably the most iconic one-day race in cycling.) This stage was the opposite of Paris–Roubaix: it didn't matter to us GC guys who won it, but we had to finish. There were still eleven days of racing to go.

A load, too, were certainly not built for it. There were sixty-kilogram climbers who no more wanted to ride cobbles than the heavyweight sprinters did the Col du Tourmalet. Everything was back to front. Most of the cobbles experts, the ones who would ordinarily be contesting the win, were suddenly totally uninterested in victory. Their job instead was to shepherd their team leaders to the safety of the finish line and the rest day to come. Oliver Naesen would be riding for Romain Bardet. Taylor Phinney and Sep Vanmarcke were protecting Rigoberto Urán. Luke was looking after Chris. The only teams who would go for the stage one hundred per cent looked like Quick-Step, Trek and – from what we'd heard – BMC for Van Avermaet. Even then, Quick-Step still had Bob Jungels riding for GC and Trek had Bauke Mollema. Would they care enough about the mere stage?

Our fuelling strategy would be critical. We knew the first fifty kilometres would be crazy. Unwrapping a rice cake and eating it while your heart was thrashing along at 150 beats per minute was not going to happen. Eating on the cobbles themselves? No chance. Between the secteurs you might get a chance if the racing eased slightly, but if you waited for these moments, you'd never make it to Roubaix. So it was a day for gels. Load up your back pockets, boys! We weren't climbing any mountains so a little extra weight wasn't going to make a difference, but relying on getting a couple of feeds was still risky. The team, along with nutritional partners SIS, had developed more concentrated carbohydrate drinks for days like these. We had our standard 'X' drink: twenty grams of carbs and some salt. There was a drink with double the amount of carbs as 'X', known as the 'Classics' drink. Then the big boy: Beta Fuel, or 'rocket fuel' as some of us nicknamed it, with a whopping eighty grams of carbs. We would still need to hydrate too. It was hot, so it would be too easy to dehydrate and then underperform. Fifteen secteurs of cobbles. Zone-hoppers in every one. Okay. At least fifteen chances to grab a bottle of water.

Advice came from unexpected sources, too. Luke's parents, both hugely keen cyclists, had come out to the north of France with their bikes. The night before, his mum had WhatsApped him a video of the two of them riding into and through the first secteur.

'Boys, do you want a look?'

'Yeah, stick it out on the team group, perfect.'

'Thing is, she's talking all the time, and it's a bit embarrassing. Does anyone know how to knock the sound off?'

'Don't worry about that, it'll be fine.'

So we all watched as Luke's parents gave us their tour, and we all listened as his mum's tips came through. 'Here we go, Luke! Goodness me, that's a tight left. Ooh, it's narrow. Dear me, this is a rough bit, Luke. Wow, look at all the caravans! How do we get over there?'

Her excitement was a joy. The race itself, straight out of Arras Citadelle just before 1 p.m., was horrific.

I'm told it was fun to watch. To ride it was insane. There were fifty kilometres before we even hit the first section of pavé, and it was the most stressful fifty kilometres of my life. It was like the last four kilometres of a bunch sprint stage spread out at the same intensity across an hour rather than five minutes. Our Garmins slowly counting down the kilometres to the first secteur and then each one after that, for before the stage we'd programmed in the route with key waypoints, the start and finish of every sector. Everyone scrapping for every tiny patch of road, Luke shouting at Movistar's Imanol Erviti, who was shouting at BMC's Michael Schär, everyone shouting at anyone within shoutable distance and barely even realising it. Guys in the wind – where you'd never usually want to be because it's much harder – fighting to stay in the wind since that was safer than being sent backwards into the churning mess. Us trying to hold our Team Sky bubble even as it was squeezed on all sides. All of it nuts, for nothing was going to happen until the first secteur, but also entirely understandable, because to be safe in that first secteur you had to be into it at the front. An hour in which you used bullets so that you could save them later. Spend energy now rather than burning through more when you were desperately chasing back after being stranded and abandoned.

It had the predictable effect. A huge crash, back behind us leaders, bikes and bodies everywhere. Richie Porte always likes to have more space around him, whether he's descending or rattling along in the pack, and when he rode with us on Sky we understood that and tried to give it to him. He's had consistently bad luck on crashes, almost more than me, and so a safety buffer around him, even if it's only a foot or two, helps keep him calm.

In this deranged race within a race within a race, you couldn't ride cautiously. You couldn't look for space because there wasn't any. You had to get involved, dive in and relish it.

There's still no television footage of him going down. One

moment he's racing, the next he's sitting on the grassy verge, clutching the right shoulder of his red and black jersey, face scrunched up in pain. A fractured collarbone, another Grand Tour over, another disaster on stage 9 of a Tour de France. At the 2015 Giro it had been mechanical issues, at the 2016 Tour, illness. Now he was being led away in tears, victim of the fear that cobbles engender before the cobbles had even begun.

Richie's a mate. We hang out. Sara is good friends with his wife Gemma, whom he met when both were at Sky, and I felt so bad for him. I knew how hard he had worked; he was the same as me with the weight struggles, finding it hard to stay low every day of every week. He had won the Tour de Suisse in the build-up to this year, and although I had seen him in better shape still, he had been one of my pre-race favourites for yellow. He had pulled hard for most of the Mûr-de-Bretagne and looked impressively strong. If anyone deserves a little luck, it's Richie. It'll happen, I'm sure. He's too good for it not to.

Cruel though it is, you cannot dwell on the misfortune of others on a stage like that. Look back and you're not looking forwards. If you're not looking forwards, then you will be the next one rolling around in the dirt and wheels.

Our tactics had come together. Get through the first three secteurs and get into them in the top fifteen to reduce the chances of being derailed by bad luck, ours or that of others. Then stay at the front of the race, which will hopefully be splitting up behind us. Don't get too carried away and start chasing every move. We hoped to still have numbers for the denouement. If we did – if me and Chris were there, with Luke and Gianni and Kwiato in support – we could maybe try something in the final thirty kilometres.

Get through the first three secteurs? Get through the first secteur. It was a wide road turning sharply into a corridor of dust and expectant, out-turned faces. Three lanes into one, smooth tarmac into dirt and cobbles. So much shouting – 'Go go go!' at teammates, something much tastier at rivals from different teams trying to dive onto your teammates' wheel. It was total chaos, handle-bars bumping handlebars, upper bodies leaning into each other, curses and yells and your heart going faster than your feet on the pedals.

It would have been bad enough for Paris–Roubaix. For a stage of the Tour, when a third of the riders had absolutely no desire to be riding cobbles and another third had abso-lutely no idea how to do so, it was a different kind of hell of the north. The mechanics tweak your bike set-up to match the conditions: a double layer of bar tape to provide a little cushioning against the relentless drill action of handlebars on palms, wrists and shoulders; wider tyres, a slightly lower tyre pressure to absorb more of the impact, although go too low and you simply puncture instead. Pinarello had also developed a new cobbles-specific bike with automatic suspension on the back forks. For most of the stage on the smoother tarmac it would be locked, but as soon as we hit the cobbles it would turn on and give us some relief. The nerves still were a constant clang, the stress making everyone behave in daft ways. 'Guys, we've got a hundred kilometres of this left!' Carnage, everywhere you looked. Romain Bardet was the first to pull over with a puncture and start waving his arms desperately for a spare wheel. Moscon was next, although our Sky helpers were easy to spot in their luminous yellow bibs, and both were able to get back to the group.

In 2015, when I had ridden at the front for Froome, that had felt much more doable. This was just Roubaix secteurs, coming thick and fast. Mitchelton-Scott team director Matt White had already said he thought it was too much. But any amount of cobbles would have brought dread. Had there only been three secteurs, maybe it would have compressed the same amount of tension into a fifth of the time. At least it wasn't wet. The heatwave that had Europe in its grip continued to show no sign of letting go.

You couldn't enjoy it, even when you enjoyed cobbles. Bodies going everywhere, chaos even out the back. Wout was ten minutes back from our lead group, and there were still guys crashing on every corner. I tried to stick to the riding techniques that had served me on cobbles in the past: hands anchored on the drops, rather than the brake hoods where they could be shaken loose; keeping shoulders as relaxed as you could rather than fighting the relentless vibrations; looking long rather than at the surface immediately in front of your wheel, so you could plot your path over the cobbles several moves in advance, like a snooker player planning four shots ahead of his current pot.

It should have felt like a stage on fast-forward. Instead it was like slow motion. That first fifty kilometres had been both flat-out and endless. No sooner had you finished thinking, 'Let's get this done . . .' then you were on the cobbles and desperate for those to be over too.

Four or five in, somewhere after the 2,000m of de War-laing à Brillon and the 2,400m of Tilloy à Sars-et-Rosières, I looked around and saw my teammates massed. Luke and Gianni riding hard, Chris tucked in, Alejandro Valverde and another couple of GC guys from other teams just behind, and then not much else. Right, a split. Let's go! Let's capitalise and take some time!

It never happened. Valverde was never going to do a turn at the front, because he had his teammates Quintana and Landa in one of the groups behind. Greg Van Avermaet was only up with us because his BMC leader Richie was already in the team car on his way to hospital. Had it been Paris–Roubaix, everyone would have chopped off. Every man for himself. Instead it was all shrugs and outstretched arms. I've got so-and-so behind, I'm sitting on here.

Usually on the cobbles the spectators are right up in your face. You can smell the beer on their breath and the meat on their barbecues. On the bergs, the short climbs in the Tour of Flanders, you can feel bare forearms and hot breath on your face as you squeeze past on the smoothest bit of road you can find. You see British and Welsh flags and you feel the kick in your legs from that marvellous travelling support.

Today I was aware of nothing. Riding those two Olympic pursuit finals on the track in Beijing and London I had been so dialled into the 4,000m of riding that I had only been conscious of a solid roar of noise. It was the same out in that heat and dust and angst. We could have been being booed on every secteur and I wouldn't have had a clue. There may have been close family friends on the roadside and I would have had no idea. I saw the odd Welsh flag when I lifted my head on the long straight, and I vaguely recall a stray British voice as I slowed round one tight corner. Such was the intensity and the concentration, that this was the day I took in least.

On we raced, Sky all in one piece, and I was beginning to think of the end, when it almost all did. On the entry to the Mons-en-Pévèle secteur, at 900 metres one of the shortest yet most feared of the day, Gianni lost his front wheel on the cobbles and came down hard on his left-hand side. Froomey, right behind him, clipped his sliding back wheel and went right over the top of his own bike. I was lucky: I'd been in front of Chris for most of the stage, but had just let him go in front of me as he was finding it hard to hold the wheel further back in the line. If I'd stayed where I was, I might have been down instead. Not again, G, not again.

There is an extraordinary photograph of the moment, taken from just in front as it all unfolds. A thin slither of sun-parched grass along the foreground of the shot, Moscon horizontal with his cheeks distending as gravity pulls the loose skin down, Froome mid-air with his arms and fingers outstretched to break his fall, face turned towards the earth. Alexander Kristoff on the right, half-crouched, half-fallen, desperately trying to wrench his handlebars round to the right even as his front wheel rolls over Gianni's back; Van Avermaet in the yellow jersey slamming on his brakes behind Froome, sweat glistening on his arms, face yet to react. Look closer and there is more – the green jersey of Peter Sagan cutting inside, Valverde grimacing and trying to swerve, a spectator in the background wearing a yellow t-shirt and an expression shifting somewhere between consternation and astonishment. Behind it all the banner heralding the start of the secteur and, beyond that still, a beautiful blue sky as calm as everything in front was mayhem.

Okay. Roll out Operation Rescue Froomey. Luke and Kwiato dropped back to pace his chase of the lead group, and with a big effort they got him back up to where I was, with Van Avermaet, the German John Degenkolb, Yves Lampaert, Philippe Gilbert and Sagan. On the very next secteur, de Mérignies à Avelin, Kwiato fell on a corner. Luke had an issue with a wheel and had to stop, and Gianni never made it back on. From two nominal leaders with three lieutenants we were suddenly down to Chris and me and not a teammate for protection in sight. Neither had all our carefully laid plans come off. Come the end of the stage, Froomey and I would shake our heads. 'Man, did your tyres feel super hard there?' 'Yeah, they did . . .' We asked our mechanic Gary to check the pressures. 6.4. '6.4! How?' Normally at the start they are around 4.5 or 5 bar – 65 to 72psi, depending on the rider. Apparently the high temperatures that day may have affected them, but by that much? Maybe that was the reason Gianni and Kwiato crashed as they did.

I can remember very little that came over the team radio. It was in my ear, but I zoned out from it amidst the focus on the real world. I can recall a terse phrase – 'Kwiato's not coming back . . .' and a few quick words from Servais. 'Next secteur in four k.' 'Ride this one down the middle, it's crap down the side.'

In Paris–Roubaix the racing is all or nothing. It's 'go!' rather than 'watch out!' If this is the best time and place to attack, you go for it – down the gutter, prepared to risk what might follow for what might yet be. If I get a puncture now, you mentally shrug, then so be it. In this Tour stage, it was less of a race than an act of completion. I was content to stay in the middle of the track working harder rather than cutting a line up the tattered inside and risking a puncture, for I had so much more to lose.

I kept the focus and kept the discipline, always holding a good position going into the pavé, racing sensibly on the tarmac. My legs felt good and the pace felt almost comfortable. When Van Avermaet, Lampaert and Degenkolb went hard somewhere around secteur twelve or thirteen, I hesitated. I was a couple of bike lengths behind; I glanced back under my arm and thought, I could follow here. But by then it was too late, the gap was there. We'd gone into the stage looking to get through it as easily as possible. This was the first day of a big block of racing – cobbles today, a flight down to the Alps, a rest day and then probably the biggest three days of mountain stages back to back that I'd ever done. Again, big picture: it's not about this stage. It's not about today. None of those three riders are capable of staying with me in the mountains next week. Why waste bullets when you have been so disciplined in the three hours thus far?

Strange things were still going on behind me. One rider seemed to have punctured at least three times yet made it back to the main group with ease on each occasion. The French television director decided not to show a second of it, which raised suspicion in several educated quarters that he had done so by sitting in the slipstream of the AG2R team car. Our three guys couldn't make it back once, yet others appeared to be enjoying a free holiday. If I'd been Tom Dumoulin, penalised for drafting three days before, I might have talked of double Dutch standards.

Still. We might have had those crashes – and Egan had time for two more, going straight through one corner before slamming into the back of a decelerating BMC car as he tried to make up lost time – but remarkably they would be the only crashes the team experienced all Tour. Not only that, but all five who hit the deck were fine to continue. Other teams would routinely lose two riders to crash-related injuries; AG2R lost four, Katusha the same. Richie had spent November through to July training for the Tour and seen it all go up in smoke with one piece of bad luck.

Up ahead, Degenkolb out-sprinted Greg and Lampaert to take a stage win that sent ripples of pleasure through the peloton. His victory wasn't entirely a surprise, although it was his debut Tour triumph; he'd won Paris–Roubaix back in 2015. It was more about what had happened since then – the accident he'd suffered in training the year afterwards when he and his Giant-Alpecin teammates were hit by a car, the trauma so severe that he had almost lost his index finger; the death of a close friend one year further on. If he was in tears at the end, there were smiles on our faces. He's not a close mate of mine; I chat to him during races, but we've never been on the same team. Yet it's always good when one of the nice guys does so well, and I was made up for him. When Sagan or Gaviria win a stage, it's 'Well done.' With Degenkolb it went much further. 'Fucking good job, mate, that's really good to see.'

I analysed it more after the finish. If I had followed, would they have ridden with me? Van Avermaet was all in for the stage, so maybe. But Lampaert had Jungels behind. Degenkolb had Mollema. Who knows? Keep it bottled, save it.

With that late break, Greg had extended his lead back to me in second place in the GC to forty-three seconds. All good. I still had nearly fifty seconds on Valverde, Rafał Majka and Jakob Fuglsang, and almost a minute on Froomey, Adam Yates and Mikel Landa. I had blisters on my hand; the skin on the right palm would be sore until mid-August. Insert your own joke about lonely nights on Tour here. But there was a sense of relief on the team bus that Froome and I had got through. Only Luke was a little disappointed: what he had thought was a puncture turned out to be a problem with his brake, meaning that when he had changed his wheel, the issue had remained. He was never going to get back up to help us then, and Luke being Luke, it left him frustrated that he couldn't work as hard as he wanted.

It was a strange sort of day, a Grand National with a lot of fallers yet an awful lot of finishers. Apart from Richie, the only other big gun to lose ground was Rigo Urán, who had crashed with around thirty kilometres to go and came home almost a minute and a half down. Landa lost only seven seconds despite a late crash when trying to take a drink; Quintana and Bardet finished in the main group, and Dan Martin – in pieces the night before – got through it as well. But there was finishing together and there was what you'd given to do so. The effort and stress that Bardet and Landa had gone through might cost them later in the race. Bardet had not so much spent bullets as thrown a couple of grenades.

I still wasn't certain we should have ridden so much pavé. You don't want the Tour decided on luck, and what else had afflicted Richie but misfortune? There had been excitement for the viewer on their sofa, but it had all come from punctures and crashing. For riders that's rubbish. That's not racing, it's surviving. Chatting to guys from other teams, most outfits seemed to have had at least four crashes. With twenty-two teams in the race, that's a lot of crashes. Egan lost fifteen minutes that day, without which he almost certainly would have ended the Tour in the white jersey of the best young rider. One crash, and his stellar performance across three weeks was irreparably damaged.

I turned my thoughts to the rest day ahead. The first half of the Tour – beaches, Brittany, wind, flat plains, crashes and cobbles – was done. The second half – the mountains, the descents, the brutal days that would truly decide the destiny of the yellow jersey – was ahead.

I was ready.

Chapter Eight

Here Come the Hills

Sometimes the Tour, to be a tour, has to bite off a whole chunk of France in one go. So it was that Sunday night: from Roubaix in the far north-east, close enough to the Belgian border to be able to smell the mayonnaise on the frites, all the way down to the shores of Lake Annecy in the Alps. Quite a few had to drive it, including most of the backroom staff, the journalists and the entire publicity caravan. It must have made for a strange sight at the autoroute payage stations when a flat-bed truck with a giant baguette on the back pulled up alongside a rented estate with one driver and three frantic typists and a saloon car with a four-metre-high fibreglass yellow jersey on the roof.

We saw none of that. We were on a plane, specially chartered, that turned out to be just as peculiar in its own way. Travel to the airport was on a communal coach, which already shattered the usual protocol. It was like getting on the bus as a kid to find three other rival schools had already taken the top deck. The plane then had no designated seating. It was like the old days of budget airlines, except – because we were cyclists – there was no scramble for the back row or the emergency exit, but instead the seats closest to the door, so you could get away with the minimal possible walking. We all still sat in teams too, which seemed rather antisocial, but I think we were still shaken by both the communal bus and the earlier cobbles. Once we settled down the atmosphere improved. It actually became quite pally and jovial, the battles of three hours before – shouting and fighting with each other for every inch of road – forgotten in one happy mid-air truce. The in-flight service, however, left a lot to be desired. No complimentary packets of salted pretzels with an undersized can of lager to wash them down, no special offers on scratch-cards or designer fragrances. Merely a bottle of water each and the understanding that we were lucky to be in the air for an hour rather than stuck in the back of a car for eight times that long.

The World Cup final was taking place as we lifted off. I watched it on my phone, supporting France because Olivier Giroud had been at Arsenal, because I had watched Kylian Mbappé at Monaco and I appreciated the team's attacking style. Plenty of the French riders were watching too, the celebrations loud at the final whistle. How sweet it would have been had England won it instead, standing up and cheering to an audience of stony-faced Gallic disapproval.

It was a satisfying feeling knowing the first rest day was upon us. I was tired but not spent, looking forward to the lack of mental angst as much as the physical rest. Twenty-four hours to chill, to sit without having to fight for position, even if the flight was as bumpy as some of those secteurs of pavé. In the same way that I could never suffer as much again on a bike as I had in my first Tour as a round-cheeked twenty-one-year-old, no turbulence could ever do to me what a trip on a twelve-seater seaplane had while on holiday in Sri Lanka. As we lurched and dropped and the world's finest cyclists tried not to scream in terror, Luke turned around laughing. 'Imagine if this plane comes down. Alpe d'Huez won't be much of a party . . .'

Privation upon privation. When we arrived at our hotel in the Alps, miles from the lakefront, right next to the motorway, our kitchen truck and chef were still chugging their way down the autoroute towards Dijon. We had to eat what was left at the dinner buffet, and man it hit home what it used to be like. Call us pampered, but I was so used to gently cooked rice, and steamed fish that retained the right amount of moisture and flavour, that I was done with in a couple of mouthfuls, 150km of cobbles or not. Lukewarm silver tureens that, by the look of their contents, could have been there for two days, something that had once been fish, salad that had turned beige where it still had colour. I went upstairs with Jonathan Castroviejo, realising as we trudged that it was close to 9.30 p.m. and the cut-off time for getting a massage. Our Polish soigneur Marek had been in the car all afternoon and evening from Roubaix. 'Ah, Castro, I'm not sure I can ask him.' A look of surprise on my teammate's usually expressionless face. 'Hey G! Second on GC, man! Massage!'

The hotel had as many flaws as floors. Apparently we had stayed there a month earlier in the Dauphiné, although I had absolutely no memory of it. Every room, every corridor, every lobby vending machine you're not allowed to touch blurs into one in the end. Our coach Tim Kerrison has recall that staggers me. 'Oh yes, this place. We stayed here on stage 3 of the Dauphiné back in 2013.' Our former Sky teammate Matt Hayman was the same. 'We've never been down this climb before, but we came up it in E3 Harelbeke four years ago. The sun was out, the wind was blowing north, north-east and the temperature was around ten to eleven degrees.'

There was a big air-conditioning unit in the corridor that I could drag into my room. Great. The summer heat was stuck in the valleys, the air heavy and humid. Air con can be a mixed blessing; the ideal temperature when you're getting into bed is significantly different to the temperature you want when you're asleep four hours later. So you wake up freezing, turn it off and then wake up an hour later sweating. Up again to turn it back on, followed by half an hour of tossing and turning because it's so loud you want to take a hammer to it.

Tonight I wanted it. We all did. Unfortunately, when all eight riders turned their units on, the power surge was so great that it cut the hotel's electricity. Consternation in the corridors, a hurried meeting of management, a message sent round on WhatsApp. 'Only one rider can have it on. That rider is Froomey.'

Right. So I'm second on GC, more than a minute ahead of Chris, and it's him who gets the cool air and good night's sleep? I knew I had only technically been a protected rider in the team for the first week, but it wasn't even midnight on the Sunday. Sometimes it's the smallest clues that tell you where you really stand.

A little realpolitik of my own. A reply: 'Okay, nice one.' A thought: 'Ah, fuck it.' A stroll back into the corridor, pushing the air-con unit back into my room, whacking it on anyway. It was so loud that I couldn't really sleep, but that was fine. For half an hour I was at the optimum temperature. When I slept after that, I only warmed up incrementally. Job done.

Rest days shake you out of your routine and monkey with your already-frazzled brain. I woke up that morning with absolutely no idea what my room number was, let alone what the outside of the hotel looked like. I wasn't even entirely sure where I was. It can take a moment or two to remember what's going on. 'Oh shit, it's the Tour!'

The itinerant life of the pro cyclist does this to you. Land at an airport and you go to collect your bag and you're looking at the board that shows what carousel to wait by, and you're thinking, where did I just fly from? Here, there and everywhere all the time. Waking up in the middle of the night needing a pee and hoping the hotel room has the standard configuration so you can find the bathroom in the dark rather than stepping through the wrong door and finding yourself in the corridor. Without your key.

A rest day is never truly a rest day, not for me. Some guys can have an actual day off, not even look at their bike, especially if they don't have to perform the next day because they're going to be sitting at the back in the gruppetto. I always feel I have to keep going – just a couple of hours getting a sweat on, a few efforts towards the end – or my body overcompensates and slips into recovery mode when I need it to kick on. Then when I try to go hard the following day, I feel absolutely terrible.

I ride even on rest days at training camps and stuff. At home I have days off, but then spend the first half of the next day trying to recover from the rest. You could compare it to the sensation when you go on holiday and seem to be far more exhausted than you were at work, because your body has realised that it can now get all that rest you were denying it for weeks. If you switch off mentally too much at a Tour, it's hard to get that focus back. It's like cutting an effort from your training plan if you're tired one day – do it once and you'll do it forever.

It's a strange sight to the uninitiated, a pack of weary riders in the middle of a three-week race who have no racing to do for once but still go out on their bikes. That crazy Roubaix stage had made it even more essential. So stressful had it been that had I done nothing I was fearful I'd get the full shutdown. We had such a hard Alpine day coming up on the Tuesday that you couldn't risk even a minor drop-off in form. What sort of insane race is it that leaves you more scared of resting than cycling up a mountain? So up a mountain we went, the Col du Chat, where Richie had crashed out on the descent the year before.

We did ninety minutes in all, with a little 'through the zones effort' – slowly ramping it up from 300 to 500 watts over ten minutes. It didn't feel nice at all but it was what I'd need to be ready for the next day. Egan was doing a similar effort in front of me; even during a little labour on a rest day I find myself assessing every pedal stroke and comparing myself to those around me, as if we were racing a stage. A quick café stop on the way home, again sparkling water instead of caffeine. A quick stop rather than a leisurely one because we'd all been sweating, and the last thing you want is to get a niggly throat after sitting around for too long and getting cold.

You still recover. The illicit air con kept me asleep until 10 a.m., a spectacular luxury. I knocked off the ride, a spot of media with Froomey, lunch and another forty-minute nap. I felt a million dollars. You become a man of simple pleasures on the Tour.

You become a man of multiple meals too. With the excesses of the cobbles just gone and a three-day block in the mountains ahead, we had to eat to recuperate and stock up. That meant more rice than I'd ever put away during the Chinese takeaways of my wide-eyed youth, washed down with hydro-juice, our sports drink with extra carbs. You notice the effect, if I can put it this way, at the other end. The volume increases, the frequency goes up. You'd describe it as anti-social, but since all eight of us on the team were going through it, none of us batted a heavy eyelid.

What I did notice was that Froomey and I were barely breaking wind at all. On a training camp, we're literally full gas. Fewer carbs, to keep the weight dropping, with much more fibre to fill you up. Here in France we weren't eating as much salad or vegetables, and the effect was instant. I could count on one hand the number of farts I had all Tour. When someone did produce a real comedic stinker on the bus, and everyone shouted, 'Who was that?' there was almost a pride in claiming it. 'Yes. Yes, that was me.'

You become relaxed about these things at the Tour. On

the Sky bus, unlike a National Express, the driver will not complain if you use the on-board toilet for both number ones and number twos. Only Gianni will refuse to go properly, and that's because there's no bidet. So Italian. I'm not even sure what he would attempt to do with one. We've got a bidet in the bathroom at our flat, and Sa uses it to clean flannels.

Stage 10 would provide, I knew, the most serious of tests. 158.5km from Annecy to Le Grand-Bornand, south along the western side of the lake to Doussard before heading north along the opposite shore and up the Col de Bluffy. A turn east into the proper high stuff – first the category 1 climb of the Col de la Croix Fry, 11.3km at an average gradient of 7%, north again, tantalisingly close to the finish but instead taking in a jagged circle up the *hors catégorie* Montée du Plateau des Glières, the 8.8km Col de Romme and then the Col de la Colombière, 7.5km at 8.5%. All these climbs were categorised in the 1950s, their grading relating to the gear that a car of that time would need to ascend them. A category 1 climb meant having to drive it in first gear. *Hors catégorie?* That meant it was so steep that a car of the era simply wouldn't be able to make it.

The Plateau de Glières would have another kick to it. Once we made the summit, we would be faced with almost two kilometres of gravel road, a return for the first time in thirty-one years to the sort of unsurfaced tracks that had once defined all the Tour's mountain expeditions. There was the possibility of it being a puncture-fest, even if its position with almost ninety kilometres still to go meant it was more about the race and the nation honouring wartime Resistance fighters who had made a famous last stand against the Nazis there, rather than a decisive shift in the GC contest.

That night I tried to leave my worries for the day itself. As a rider you spend as much time lying on your bed as you can, regardless of whether you are actually sleeping. A solid Wi-Fi connection, a tablet and a Netflix login, and life is sweet. I'd started watching a show called *Power*, based on the life of 50 Cent: drug-dealing and gangs and acts of random violence. Sa and I had an agreement in place that neither of us would sneak ahead and independently watch episodes of shows that we had been watching together. If we did, we had a term for it: Netflicked. Usually the bigger issue was allowing spoilers from other sources to leak into conversations, which meant steering clear of Sa's mum, Beth. Sit down to watch *Saving Private Ryan* with Beth, and suddenly she'll clap her hands in recognition. 'Oh, is this the one where they save Private Ryan but Tom Hanks dies?'

Cobbles send tremors through the peloton but so too do big climbs. As we pedalled gently out of Annecy that Tuesday morning, Mikel Landa and Fernando Gaviria managed to ride into a couple of plastic bollards and took tumbles so slow-motion and unnecessary that it was almost comical. It was a day when plenty of riders fancied getting in the break, for there was a good chance the break would survive. There wasn't likely to be a big GC battle, not with the long descent to the finish and two mountain top finishes to come. There was also the unknown of who would ride. BMC had yellow, but it was on Van Avermaet's shoulders, and he wasn't a GC contender, so there was no guarantee they'd ride. They'd lost their GC guy, Richie, on the road to Roubaix. All this added to the tension in the group and the crush at the front. When the flag did drop, the attacks began immediately, and it was Julian Alaphilippe who kick-started the move that stuck. Peter Sagan went with him, hunting the points on offer at the intermediate sprint, and on the Col de Bluffy, the yellow jersey of Greg Van Avermaet joined them.

I'd guessed Greg might go for it. When he'd been in yellow before he'd made similar moves to hang on to it, and although some were talking me up in the media as the man who would take the lead that day, I was in no rush. There was no one else from the top fifteen in that break, or we would have chased it down. And when it's a thirty-man break you can control it from the rear anyway; it's too many cooks to work together on the breakaway broth. Even if there are a few strong climbers in there, inevitably there will be just as many who merely want to sit on. In the flat roads of the valleys, they're not going to ride together either. Controlling thirty riders is easier than eight.

The scenery was spectacular, or so I remembered from my recons. I cared today only about the road and ride in front of me, the next wheel up or ten metres further on. I may as well have been on a turbo-trainer wired to Zwift. Coming into the villages early on the route, the streets booby-trapped with speed-bumps and traffic-calming chicanes, you cannot be looking up at the picturesque peaks all around. It's looking out for the right hand of the rider in front of you suddenly going out, or for the police outrider parked up blowing his whistle and frantically pointing left with his triangular flag. We were going round steep corners five abreast. In that formation, the man cooing over views of chocolate-box wooden chalets is the one who becomes an inadvertent bowling ball amid ninepins.

So total is your focus on the race and its tactics and permutations that you often haven't got much of a clue where you are. For smaller races, you have no idea where you're flying into until the flight details appear in Dropbox just before you set off for the airport. You get picked up on landing by the team, you get driven to the hotel. You end up as the best-travelled person you know with the least photographs. If someone had asked me to play a cycling version of the old parlour game Pin the Tail On the Donkey that week by spreading a map of France out in front of me and asking me to locate iconic Tour locations, I would have begun confidently with Roubaix and Alpe d'Huez and then tailed off fast. If you'd shown me a regional map of the Alps that morning, I wouldn't have had a clue. I didn't need to, either. I knew how many metres we would have to ascend. I had recce'd the big climbs and trained to match their challenges. Their gradients and the attacks that would come on them were what mattered, not where they happened to be.

Half the team had ridden the entire stage a month before after the Dauphiné. Kwiato and I had done the last two climbs. The info on the gravel section had been that it wasn't too bad, it was pretty smooth and compact. And it was, and although Froome punctured, took a wheel from Castro and realised that was punctured too, there were still no dramas. Luke was controlling the pace at the front of the peloton; we slowed it up, Chris got a bike change and tagged back into the group in the valley that followed. Had Castro not been with him, I wouldn't have had to drop back to help, ceding my own position; our entire team was riding, there was heaps of time before the finish.

Nothing about the team's internal pecking-order had been publically discussed. I accepted Chris was still the team leader. You'd have to have been delusional or a maniac not to. He had six Grand Tour wins under his belt, I had none. I concentrated on my own legs and form. It had been two weeks now since I'd done a proper long climb; the Mûr-de-Bretagne was a different beast. I wasn't entirely sure how my body would react, I wasn't certain how any of us would climb. You have your place in the peloton in the first week on those northern roads but it's completely different when you start going seriously up. It was almost like starting the Tour again. For now, we rode as a team, Egan Bernal tremendously strong on the climbs, Chris looking comfortable, Kwiatkowski there on every pedal stroke.

Up ahead, the break held a seven-minute advantage as they went up the Col de Romme, and after Direct Énergie's Rein Taaramäe made a move of his own, Alaphilippe kicked across to him. Those two held a lead of forty-five seconds over Van Avermaet and the rest of their group as they began the descent. All that was fine with us. Alaphilippe was chasing the King of the Mountains jersey, not the GC. I liked him, and the French television directors were gobbling up his flamboyance and clowning for their cameras. He was a strong rider excelling for Quick-Step, a super-strong team. As long as he struggled in time trials, however, he would be no danger to the yellow jersey. The time gaps in the mountains over the past few Tours have been restrained compared to the impact of the time trials. It's no longer enough to try to limit your losses against the clock. You have to be able to compete.

On days like this, we ride as a team. Castro kept the pace strong as we paced our way up the Romme, Wout and Kwiato took over as we chased up the Colombière, Alaphilippe left Taaramäe behind and Egan took over for the final kilometre or so.

Dan Martin had a dig over the top. Egan was looking really good and held him at fifty metres. He looked behind as we were cresting the climb and I gave him the nod to close it. He squeezed and Dan was back. Once the team is on a roll, everything just seems to happen. If one of the guys isn't feeling the best, someone else steps right in. We are all dialled into how we want to ride. It was almost the most impressive thing about Egan, other than his obvious talent of being able to go uphill fast. He just stepped right into that role and understood what was needed to be done. I started hearing on the radio of other riders being dropped behind us – Valverde, Rigo Urán, then Bob Jungels as the pace told in the final kilometre of the climb. Bauke Mollema, Rafał Majka and Ilnur Zakarin were also getting distanced. As that news filtered through, I was still feeling comfortable. Good. We're in business here.

On the descent, Egan was a young bull at a gate. His first mountain stage in a Tour, leading Froomey and me over the top of the final climb, nullifying other GC threats. Down the final descent, he probably just got a bit excited, wanting to go as fast as he could. On a couple of hairpins he came in a little hot, locked up his back wheel and began the start of a skid. I gave myself a bit of breathing room behind him just in case and shouted a warning into the wind in Italian – *'Occhio!'* – even though he's Colombian and I'm Welsh. The word is a familiar one around the peloton, and it was easier than 'Look out!' in English, where he might be thinking, what does that mean? And then bump – gone.

Alaphilippe, as he does, descended beautifully to take the stage win. Van Avermaet came in fourth, a minute and forty-four seconds behind Alaphilippe and one minute thirty-nine ahead of us in the peloton. That bumped his lead over me in the GC up to two minutes twenty-two seconds. De rien. It would have been nice to have taken the yellow jersey but it meant I could get to the Sky bus without hassle or delay, be significantly more chilled, have a recovery drink and enjoy my shower. When you hold the race lead, you don't shower until you get to your hotel two hours later. You can change your shorts but your skin is still sticky with dried sweat. Anyway, as a team we were in control.

Had I never worn yellow before I might have gone after it a little more, been a bit more stressed about it, wasted more energy thinking about it. That night, I knew Greg's had been a last hurrah. I couldn't be certain what was next for me, but I felt good, and I knew too that some of the other big boys had not found the transition from cobbles to climbs as straightforward as I had. Jungels, Majka, Zakarin and Mollema had all shipped fifty-one seconds. Poor old Rigo had lost significantly more. Even if I had something of a bad day up La Rosière on Wednesday, I should still be able to take it. It's the yellow jersey in the Tour de France; it's not every day you get the chance to grab it. But stick to the plan. Big picture. This was only the first of six serious mountain days. Keep doing everything right. Don't look too far ahead.

I could take confidence from how I had ridden. I had the legs for the mountains. Now I could get stuck in and see what happened.

Tim Kerrison

Head of Athlete Performance, Team Sky

Probably the most impressive training sessions I've seen G do have been in early-season camps, in 2018 with the Australian triathlete Cameron Wurf in Los Angeles, and in Crystal Springs, South Africa, with Chris Froome in 2017.

We call very long, high-intensity aerobic efforts 'SAP' (Sustained Aerobic Power) efforts. In the three weeks G was in LA, he did three big sessions. These always started with a two-hour SAP effort on his time-trial bike, up and down the Pacific Coast Highway. In the best of these efforts, he covered ninety-two kilometres in two hours. He would then change onto his road bike, and do another couple of hours of climbing efforts in the Santa Monica mountains. In his training block at altitude in South Africa with Chris, the most memorable training day – one they still talk about – was a four-hour, two-man SAP effort on road bikes. They covered 160km in four hours, in the mountains.

These sessions would be the last day of a big three- or four-day training block, when they may not have been fresh enough to do really good quality, short, high-intensity efforts, but could still manage to grind out very impressive long, sustained efforts. It's this type of training, typically done early season, that helps both to develop the condition required to endure the hard training that will follow later in the season. It also develops the endurance required to perform in the conditions and at the moments that matter in a Grand Tour – under the accumulated fatigue of a three-week race, at the end of a five-hour stage, in the heat, at altitude.

The May training camp on Mount Teide in Tenerife was the most important big training block leading into the Tour de France. The mountainous terrain, great roads, heat and altitude all made it the perfect training environment, and the presence of most of the Tour team together in the same location gave us a unique opportunity to simulate and rehearse the way we wanted to ride in the race – not just the physical demands, but also, importantly, communication.

We might start at the bottom of the mountain with eight riders, with the objective of delivering G to the top of the mountain, twenty kilometres up the road. Just like in a race, we'd start with a rough plan, based on our knowledge of what each rider could do, but part of the exercise was for the riders to communicate with each other and adapt the plan accordingly. We would start with the rouleurs emptying the tank on the lower slopes, always at the perfect pace for the leader. Then the middle-mountain guys would take over, followed by the pure climbers, who would then lead out G into the final one or two kilometres. Then he would be on his own to the top.

Just like in a race, the objective was to use the team to protect the leader as much as possible, for as long as possible, but still get him up the climb as fast as possible. Sometimes these sessions went horribly wrong, usually when communication broke down and the team didn't adapt, but that was a precious lesson for the team. And when they went to plan, that well-executed team effort gave the whole team a sense of achievement and confidence – in their own individual performance, in their teammates. With Froome away racing at the Giro, G was leader in a number of great team efforts in the April and May Tenerife camps in 2018, finishing at over 2,000m altitude. Going into the twin summit-finish stages of La Rosière and Alpe d'Huez, I knew he was perfectly set up.

Chapter Nine

Yellow

Wednesday, 18 July. Stage 11, taking us in 108.5km and just over 3 hours of racing eastwards across the Savoie Alps from Albertville to La Rosière, a few miles short of the Italian border. It was a Leo Messi of a stage – short, but full of the sort of tricks that could destroy the unwary opponent: an early zigzag up the Montée de Bisanne, 12.4km at an average gradient of 8.2%; a 1,000m plummet down to Beaufort, then back up the Col du Pré, a new climb for the Tour with some familiar teeth, 12.6km at 7.7%. A little technical descent then up Cormet de Roselend to a height of 1,968m, right up in the clouds, followed by a rapid descent of 1,110m and then the final assault up to the ski resort at La Rosière. 17.6km at 5.8%, but that average gradient hid all manner of ramps and punches. People come on holiday to the Alps to relax, convalesce and marvel at the scenery. We had not.

Monday's rest day had brought the first stirrings of media interest in the relationship between Chris Froome and me. We had spoken about our respective positions early in the first week, when he lost time in his crash, and he seemed relaxed about it all, not least because he hadn't lost time on several others – Richie Porte, Nairo Quintana, Adam Yates.

It's good for you, G, had been the message. The boys in the team should be able to get us both to the finale of the race, and we know on the big mountain stages we can ride together until the last few kilometres. You've got a good chance of being on the podium come Paris, and we should get you there if we can.

It wasn't meant to be patronising and I didn't take it that way. I was happy to be in second and happy to be the leading Sky rider in the general classification, and I wanted to keep my lofty position for as long as possible. But if push came to shove and I had to ride for Chris instead, then I was absolutely prepared to. That was the cause. That was what we had all signed up to. And it was a meritocracy; across the past six years, Chris had won four of the last five Tours de France.

The two of us had always lived close to each other, first when we were both based in Italy with Barloworld and later in Monaco. We have trained together for years, both on team camps and big blocks in South Africa. We're good mates, although Chris is not someone you tend to socialise with. He's not someone who goes for food or organises a meal out with the boys. Which is fine – you don't have to dine with every colleague from work to like them or admire their talents. He's also hardly home, and I'm often away at different races and camps, so our schedules seldom overlap. Though to be fair, we are away together so often, it's nice to spend time with your actual wife when you're home.

I had seen first-hand his remarkable fortitude, how much he wanted to win. That determination, more than any specific physical attribute, was his greatest strength. It drove everything else. He seldom appeared to let the external noises break his calm, or at least never let it bleed into his disposition or behaviour. The atmosphere around the team dining table on the Tour tends to be set by the team leader. Brad Wiggins could be either the life and soul of the evening or almost monosyllabic. You could find yourself tiptoeing around his moods: are we going to get Happy Brad tonight, with all his impersonations and jokes, or Silent Brad?

Chris is always the same Chris at the table. Never super quiet and never super chatty, just considered, polite; a much more stable presence. It makes him easier to deal with, because you always know where you stand. If he was pissed off, you knew he was going to say something. When Brad was quiet, you didn't know if he was angry at something or just tired.

I'd learned from Chris too. When I had seen him on the podium, with the media, I'd watched how he had grown into the undisputed team leader once Brad's star had started to fade. He in turn had studied how Brad had coped with the intensity of leading the Tour, and all the extra responsibilities and demands it brings. I wanted to be on top of that podium too, but the motivation was only about the riding at the heart of it all. I had never looked for the recognition or money or free stuff that Froomey might have got and thought, that's what I want. I only cared for what triggered it all: winning stages, being at the front going into the last few kilometres of a punishing summit finish, out-kicking my rivals when none of us really had anything left to give. The accolades and aftermath never even figured.

You take what you can from each other and you use each other to fuel that desire. Much of our form for these big mountain days came from our training camps together on Mount Teide on Tenerife, endless long climbs and reps designed by Tim Kerrison to make us suffer in the moment so we could flourish in July. There had been one day in February where the weather had been more Cardiff than Canarian, sleet coming in sideways. I still went out riding with Wout Poels for four hours, with a big ninety-minute effort in the middle hitting exactly the number of watts that Tim had stipulated. Froomey had chosen to do an hour-long session on the stationary trainer instead. When he saw me staggering back into the hotel, sodden and exhausted, he shook his head. 'You boys have done what you needed to. I haven't.' He ended up getting his bike out and going out on the road at four o'clock in the afternoon, dragging Tim out with him to follow in the team car. I would have done exactly the same thing in his cleats. That's why the binary idea that a few people in the media were putting about of us being rivals never rang true. We had the form we did in part because of each other.

Two more two-week training camps on Teide had followed that first one. While the hotel at the top of the old volcano where we stayed was at altitude, it was the training we got through and the food we didn't that made me optimistic about my chances on this stage and the following day up Alpe d'Huez. I knew from experience that I would come out of each fortnight better than I went in: the first camp about low-intensity efforts, the second stepping up the volume of riding, the third, when your fitness was at good-enough-to-cope, high intensity and long rides. It wasn't unusual to ride for six hours a day. In one week I was in the saddle for a cumulative thirty-seven hours. That's a decent timesheet for an office job sat at a desk and computer.

I'd flown from that last camp to the Alps to ride the week-long Critérium du Dauphiné as my last stage race before the Tour. The Dauphiné works because it takes in so many of the same roads that the Tour will a few weeks later. We had even ridden a stage that almost exactly replicated this one up to La Rosière, and it was the manner of my victory in that race, as much as the win itself, which made me wonder just how good my form might be. I may not have won an individual stage but I always felt in control, punchy on the climbs, strong where others were evidently suffering. I even managed to crash on the prologue in Valence, get back on and lose only twenty-one seconds. Man, I thought, I'm absolutely flying . . .

As we rolled out of Albertville, I made an effort not to think too much about the consequences of that form. The talk was all around – you could end up taking the yellow jersey today, you might not even have to race for it, it could come to you by default. I understood only too well that you can take nothing for granted at a Tour. Who knew what accidental traps and misfortunes lay up there in the hills? A break could get away. Someone could nick it by a few seconds. Don't chase it, G, let it come to you.

Sure enough the big break went early. Peter Sagan, the great accumulator as well as the habitual showman, picking up his green jersey points at the early intermediate sprint, Julian Alaphilippe kicking at the summit of the Montée de Bisanne to tighten his own grip on the polka-dot jersey. It was more about the almost-invisible others chasing him that mattered to us – Søren Kragh Andersen, from Tom Dumoulin's Sunweb team; Mikel Landa, Alejandro Valverde and Quintana's Movistar teammate Marc Soler; Adam Yates' Mitchelton-Scott men Mikel Nieve and Damien Howson; Dan Martin and UAE Team Emirates' Colombian climber Darwin Atapuma. Those men were there as advance parties for their GC riders. If one of the big boys could wriggle away from the pack, the man parachuted ahead could drop back and tow him away. On his own, the big name would be easily chased down. With a teammate, he could possibly escape for good.

Luke Rowe spots these things and adjusts our outlook and pace accordingly. On the Col du Pré, Movistar got on the front and cranked the pace up a little more. Greg Van Avermaet was the first to drop back, his well-deserved time in the sun gone for another year; then Luke, his work done. Rigo Urán was next, then Bauke Mollema. It was what mountains always did to us: hunt out the weak, separate them from the strong, cast them aside.

Valverde attacked with a sudden acceleration. It had been coming, with Soler in place up the road. I watched him go and hoped no others from the peloton would jump out to join him. If it was just him, the odds were still in our favour.

Valverde has had an extraordinary career, including a two-year doping ban and a remarkable late-career renaissance. But it takes a lot of energy going that early. There were still fifty-five kilometres left for him to survive. At the Giro you might get away with it, because it's a race of strong individuals rather than teams packed with superstars, but the wild gamble is more likely to pay off when the race is harder to control. Had Valverde's move brought a rush of other flutters from those eyeing yellow jerseys, it would have been a far bigger worry.

It still wasn't great. By the Cormet de Roselend, he and Soler had almost two minutes on us. That made him the virtual race leader on the road. We had opted to let him go; we didn't want to go too deep as a team, and maybe lose a couple of guys just to keep him in check. You also trust that other teams will be equally concerned about it. So it was that Bahrain-Merida started to work at the front so that their leader Vincenzo Nibali wouldn't lose too much time either. You can plan for a great deal, but the happy accidental alliance is just as good as anything hatched weeks in advance. That two-minute lead was soon cut in half.

Eighteen kilometres of descending ahead before the long final climb. Attacks usually come when the road rears up but they can come when it drops away too. Jonathan Castroviejo was third man in our chase group, me fourth wheel. When Castro just dropped fractionally off the rear wheel of the man in second, Dumoulin and his teammate Kragh Andersen went off like an express train. There was little initial stress. Then it became clear that Kragh Andersen was going full gas. Pretty quickly they had thirty seconds on us. That was stress.

Right. That's Valverde up the road with a teammate, that's Dumoulin – second to Froome at the Giro in May, winner of it the year before – off and away with backup, too. Valverde was dropping back as the final climb began, but that only meant Dumoulin had another man to work with, too. That subtly altered the landscape once more. With the real steep stuff still to come, so much could change. Dumoulin might make a good target for me to chase across to. It could also be hugely dangerous. The group further up the road – Warren Barguil, Michael Valgren, Mikel Nieve, a pair of Cofidis riders and a few others – could do what they wanted. The stage was theirs to scrap over. All that mattered was the relative placing of the GC riders.

Egan Bernal was having a tough day. It's going to happen when you're twenty-one and in your first Grand Tour. He had also put in a veteran's shift twenty-four hours earlier on the road to Le Grand-Bornand. It was searingly hot, and the air was thin. Kwiato saw this and took on the burden himself. It's what has to happen on big blocks of mountain stages. Domestiques, even of the super variety, need a little help themselves every now and then.

You could split the climb to La Rosière into three. The first third averaged around 5%; the next third kicked up at closer to 9%, as it cut its way in sharp lines and switchbacks up the mountain. The final third settled back down to 5%. I wondered what we would all have in our legs come then.

Up ahead, Soler was done. That left Kragh Anderson to give Dumoulin and Valverde one final pull before he too peeled away. It would have suited Tom a treat had Alejandro then shared the burden with him as he looked to push on, but that's when the cruel zero-sum game of the Tour's Alpine climbs comes into play. Valverde could shrug and point out that he had Quintana and Landa back down the road. Why should he work to put time into them?

I heard on the team radio that our old Sky buddy Nieve had broken away on his own at the front of the race. Good old Frosty, a great teammate, a nice man. His move also told us that his Mitchelton-Scott team leader Adam Yates was cooked for the day. You can't accelerate away if there's a chance your GC man could use you to stay in touch.

On to the steepest part of the mountain, the crowds yelling and gesticulating on either side of the road, Kwiato was riding well and Dumoulin had such a tempo thirty seconds up the road that Valverde was spat out too. So much for his great gamble.

Patches of sunlight and shade on the road, questions forming in my mind. Kwiato's tempo was good, but he would soon be spent. I could see him rocking, about to swing over. 'A little more, mate! Come on!' I needed everything out of him. Once he was out, it would leave just Froomey and me of the original Sky phalanx. I didn't want to just ride on the front and set the tempo as I'd always done. It's what everyone expected, and it would take a lot more out of me than our rivals. I was the highest-placed GC man left on the road. Van Avermaet was miles away.

The yellow jersey was there to be taken. Nieve had a one-minute lead over Dumoulin with six kilometres to go. Chris and I were about thirty-five seconds further back. Quintana, Nibali, Martin, Romain Bardet and Primož Roglič were all in close order.

I didn't really think about it too much. Pure instinct, wrapped up in the moment, the racing part of my brain firing out the signal to attack. Go. Go. Go . . .

I was surprised how easily I left them all behind. It wasn't an all-out attack where you give it full gas to close a critical gap. It was relatively controlled and steady, a paced effort rather than super deep. And it worked, beautifully. Behind me, they all waited for each other. Up ahead, Tom was in the distance and then suddenly I was on him, able to sit on his wheel because I knew that he knew that I had Froome behind, and we both knew that I couldn't work with a rival of both of ours to stick the knife into my undisputed – for now – team leader.

Tom would be strong once the gradient eased back out to 5%-ish. It was perfect for his time-trialling way of riding mountains: maintaining a constant effort, never surging into the red, firing only the bullets that could do real damage. On the radio I could hear stress in Froome's voice: 'G. Don't go through. Don't give him a turn.' I wasn't going to, anyway, but I could sense the slightest edge of panic.

The next element of my plan was formulating in my mind. Just sit on Tom until the final kilometre and then go, try and put a bit of time into him at the death. Take this opportunity to do as much damage to my rivals as I could.

Chris followed one attack from Bardet and then jumped on another from Dan Martin. Perfect. Dan could tow him up, save Chris's legs. Quintana, Nibali and Roglič looked at each other and waited for someone else to follow. No one did. That was them gone.

It wasn't until the final 1,500m that I spotted Nieve in my peripheral vision, just a glimpse of his slate grey and yellow jersey on one of the hairpins up ahead. I was feeling great, ready to launch the same final attack I'd used on the same road in the Dauphiné a month earlier. Maybe I could catch him. Maybe this could be yellow, and a little bit more on top.

Bang. Away from Tom, smooth again but a lot deeper than before, a ninety-second effort, strong all the way to the line, all the stuff I'd trained for on Teide. Frosty coming back to me like a man on elastic, a man who had properly blown. He was treading water. I had time to feel sorry for him as an old teammate and friend, and then I was past him. And I flew past him as well.

A sprint all the way through to the line, full out now, cutting the apex of the final few bends. The first big release of emotion as I looked back to see nothing behind me and looked ahead to see the line, lonely and lovely and waiting just for me.

Fuck, I'm going to win the stage.

I'm going into yellow.

A yell, a clench of the fists. Come on!

So that's what a summit finish win feels like. So that's what it's like to ride away from the best racers in the world.

Tour winners, Giro champions, Vuelta heroes. Your own teammates and team leader.

When I dreamt as a kid of riding The Tour, I never really thought about winning. It was about racing as well as I could, about being there in the final reckoning. Riding wheel to wheel with the top guys and then racing the last few yards.

I pulled over and unclipped my feet from the pedals, the sloped roofs of the village's chalets spread out down the steep slopes to my left and up across the hillsides above. Television cameras around me, and then my soigneur with a drink. Breathing deeply, all the emotion wanting to spill out, trying not to get carried away. Whoa. That hadn't been a full-out attack, the one that had distanced them – it was hard but it wasn't everything I had, and yet it had been enough, and when I had kicked off Dumoulin, he hadn't been able to go with me ...

I was almost thrown by how comfortable it had been, from when I had been in the wheels, earlier on the stage and in the initial sections of the final climb, to where I now stood. I'd been thinking that there must be a good few other guys feeling like this. I was the strongest in the Dauphiné, but this was the Tour. Everyone must have improved. There's got to be a few feeling like me.

Except there didn't seem to be. When I saw the highlights later that night of the moment I had attacked, you could see the guys jumping around the group, but no one really had the legs to keep it going. They would try a little attack and then sit back. And watching Froomey, I could tell he was worried when I was going away. There had been the message over the radio, telling me not to work with Dumoulin; there was an urgency to the way he was riding. A couple of attacks, but nothing telling and nothing like what I'd seen him do so many times in the decisive kilometres of a summit finish.

Chris and Tom had come in twenty seconds back on me. Dan Martin had lost twenty-seven seconds. The next group – Quintana, Nibali, Roglič, Bardet – were almost a minute down.

The damage wasn't decisive but it was deep. Mikel Landa a minute and forty-seven seconds down. Valverde three, Yates and Jakob Fuglsang getting towards five. Rigo, Rafał Majka and Bauke Mollema were a full ten minutes back.

Yellow. Yellow by a distance. I was topping the GC by a minute and twenty-five seconds from Froomey and a minute and forty-four seconds from Dumoulin in third. Nibali was two minutes and fourteen seconds back, Roglič two minutes thirty-three seconds. Landa and Bardet were nearly three minutes off, Martin and Quintana just over.

It all changes when you're in yellow. You stand on the podium and look out over the fans and the cameras and the barriers and bikes, and they zip you into the jersey with its fastening at the back like the most welcome straitjacket in the world. You shake hands with every local dignitary well-connected enough to have made it onto the front of the stage and then those well-connected enough to get backstage, and then your soigneur squirts antibacterial hand gel onto your upturned palms when they're not looking so you can make sure that their well-wishes are not joined by a cough or sneeze or backdoor issue that could accidentally bring all that perfect physical conditioning crashing down.

I did try to soak it up and really enjoy it. I was older and wiser. The reverses of the past had taught me that these things don't happen every day. If I needed any more reminding of how cruel the sporting life can be, it was there at the start and end of the stage. There had been news on my phone as we had left the team hotel that Sam Warburton, captain of the Wales rugby team and the British and Irish Lions, another ex-pupil (like me and Gareth Bale) of Whitchurch High School, had been forced to retire at twenty-nine with an injury. Then news, as I finished my stage winner's press conference in a temporary marquee, that Mark Cavendish, my old housemate, the man our Great Britain team had helped pilot to the world road race title in Copenhagen in 2011, had finished outside the time cut for the day and been eliminated from the race.

Cav had endured a tough year, derailed by repeated crashes and, eventually, the diagnosis that his Epstein-Barr virus had returned. While some were bemoaning the end of his Tour – a second in succession without a stage win, when he had thirty in the bank and needed only four more to draw level with Eddy Merckx at the top of the all-time Tour lists – I saw instead the same talented, stubborn kid who I had ridden with at the British Academy for so long, and the same British Academy refusal to give in that Rod Ellingworth had bred into all of us.

He could have climbed off his bike at any point on

those final two climbs, well away from the crowds and the photographers. More than a few of the other exhausted sprinters did. He was never going to finish within the time limit. But he finished it because we boys always finish it, and Rod stayed back for an hour to see him home, even though Cav hasn't been with Sky for years and Rod had no official responsibility for him anymore.

That night, at dinner in our hotel, we celebrated with a glass of champagne. One each, albeit a small one, and not everyone took more than a sip or two from theirs, but still. There would have been a time when a summit finish win at the Tour would have been enough for me. Cycling doesn't forget you after you've won a stage up an iconic mountain. You will be a name in the sport until you're done.

Cycling also never stops. That's the thing with the Tour. There's always the next day. There's always something else – another stage, another climb, another battle to be fought. Live in the moment for as long as you can and enjoy what you have just achieved, but hold back the reins on the excitement. Stay calm. Keep with the mindset that has worked so well for you across the first ten days.

This is not just about now. This does not finish here.

Chapter Ten

The Alpe

You can feel form on the bike and you can feel form when you get up in the morning too. You don't dance out of bed but you definitely notice that you're not completely screwed. After a night's sleep, you think, I'm refreshed again now. When you start the day, your legs work. The soreness is there but it's not overwhelming.

That Thursday morning, I didn't think about the fact that I would be swapping my white and black Sky jersey for a pristine yellow one. I just walked from the bed in my small hotel room to the bathroom and thought, I feel good here. There's more to come.

When the form isn't there, then neither is your mood. When you're tired from training, the grumpiness arrives as you get off your bike and gets worse when you realise you can't eat what you'd actually like to eat. You get home and crash out on the sofa and want to turn the telly on and not talk to anyone for a couple of hours. When you finally do have food, the sleepiness takes hold, and I turn into my dad after the family Sunday lunch and start snoring in my chair. When I'm doing well in training, I'm more talkative. I'm a nicer person to be around. I'm happy that I'm doing well and the workload isn't making me so exhausted.

You look too at how your teammates feel. Breakfast was never going to be all laughs and backslapping, not after two tough days in the mountains and with a tougher one to come. Stage 12 was both an Alpine classic and a new twist on an old form of torture: 175.5km from Bourg-Saint-Maurice to Alpe d'Huez, 72 of those kilometres uphill, spiking its way south-west across the most beautifully horrible climbs the organisers could find. Three *hors catégorie* ascents, first the Col de la Madeleine, 25km long at an average gradient of more than 6%, then the Croix de Fer via its nastiest option, 29km at 5% with a summit at 2,000m, and finally the big daddy of them all – Alpe d'Huez, 13.8km at an average of 8%, each of its 21 hairpins named after a previous Tour stage winner there, every one rammed with fans who had arrived days in advance and barely stopped drinking since. In case we felt in some way bored, there was also the Lacets de Montvernier, a comparative tiddler at 3.4km but still an assault on the legs and lungs at 8%, a ridiculous road that did indeed resemble a pair of shoelaces draped up a mountain and looked as delightful on television as it was painful to ride.

5,000m of height for us to gain. That sort of menu brings a smile to no one's face over their morning espresso and omelette. It was secretly quite uplifting when Michał Kwiatkowski quietly mentioned that he was tired, that yesterday had been a big day, and equally as important that I didn't vocalise the thought going through my own head: I didn't think it was too bad. You can't crack the morale of your own teammate, whether it's accidental or otherwise. Partly because it would be cruel, and partly because they'd probably think you were a right dick. And they'd be right.

Alpe d'Huez was a mountain that even people who didn't like cycling had heard about. The cliché says that it is to riding your bike what Lord's is to cricket or Wembley to football. The difference is the ordinary punter can never canter in from the Pavilion End to bowl at Lord's nor run out of the tunnel at Wembley and dribble a ball across the pitch. Anyone with a bike and a little courage can ride Alpe d'Huez, or at least have a crack at it. Thousands would be doing exactly that as we made our way out of Bourg-Saint-Maurice. Thousands more would have made pilgrimages earlier in the summer or long after we had gone.

As a kid it seemed impossibly far away to me. We never had a family holiday in France or a special trip out to catch a stage. We didn't travel from south Wales to the south coast of England when the Tour popped briefly over in 1994; I was only eight and hadn't even discovered bike racing then. The closest I got was going to see the Amstel Gold race in the far north of mainland Europe one spring. I was thrilled to find out one year that the old Pru Tour was supposed to finish by the City Hall in Cardiff, but the stage ended up getting cancelled after a serious accident. Instead Chris Boardman, its big homegrown star, came to do a little speech for those who had assembled in vain. At the time I really appreciated the effort he had made. When I made the grade myself, I reminded myself of what Chris had done and the effect it had on me. Maybe a few people now looked up to me in the same way, and little gestures that I made might also have a disproportionally large impact.

I had loved watching the Tour's half-hour highlights each night on Channel 4. Even the notion of a Briton riding it seemed outlandish. You might have Boardman shining in the prologue, or later David Millar, but it appeared that you had to be superhuman to ride and succeed. I had no idea how you'd even begin, beyond guessing that you'd have to go to live abroad and commit yourself totally to an entirely different existence. As a family, we started going away on summer holidays to Majorca. That seemed like a whole other world, and the Tour was a million miles further on from that.

Only when I started winning races as a junior did the notion that it might somehow one day feature me start to seem in any way possible. I began to realise that there was a chance I could turn professional At some stage. But the mountains? The mountains always seemed ridiculous. When you grow up in Britain, the concept of a road so steep it required 21 hairpins is an impossibility. What did 2,000m even look like?

When I was in the Welsh junior squad, our coach Darren Tudor took us back to Majorca, this time for a training camp. The size of the climbs astonished me. The descents went on forever. So this is what it's like! I'd hit every descent full gas. I was like a kid who had obsessed about theme parks suddenly being allowed to run free on every ride as much as he liked. It was the same when I got to ride cobbles for the first time. Discomfort and trepidation on the faces of others, sheer happiness on mine. I'm on cobbles! Even now when we do our recons on the *pavé* I'm the kid from Birchgrove who can't believe he's doing a section of Paris–Roubaix. I want to turn every secteur into a flat-out sprint. And the mountains had so much more – not just the terrain but the sunshine, the wispy clouds drifting around in the valleys below, the fans drinking and dancing, thick around the handlebars of the riders doing their slow-motion dance on the pedals, the flags hanging over the road, the flares and the smoke and the constant honking of the police motorbikes and team cars.

As a pro rider the old thrill was still there, but so too were the sober calculations. My approach to the Alps in this week had been to treat them as a three-day block. It was no use taking a glorious solo win one day if it destroyed you for the next. The priority, although it lacked glamour on the surface, was not to lose time to the other GC guys. Don't spend more energy than you have to. I mentioned it to Sa that morning: 'Wouldn't it be great to have the same advantage this time tomorrow?' If I could go for a stage win in a sprint then I should go for it. As it turned out, my attack the previous day hadn't involved too much detailed thinking. It was just 'Go!' Maybe that did mean firing a few more bullets, but maybe too everyone else had done the same. I was just able to go faster.

Thursday was always going to be the biggest one. The one everyone was thinking about. There were too many opportunities to hurt your rivals, too many repeated efforts not to cast many adrift. You can be strong and able to climb and get over one great mountain in touch with the climbers, but having to ride your bike uphill for close to three hours over the mountains before one huge forty-minute effort was a test of a different magnitude. Everyone breaks at some point. No matter how much you might want it, you need the training and you need the ability and the form.

There are still plenty of whispers about how temporary my time in yellow might be. The usual stuff – it's G, he can't race well for a full three weeks, it's G, he's going to crash. The logical – Froome always comes good in the mountains. The recent precedent: G's just keeping the jersey warm for his actual team leader; it'll be like the Giro, they'll have planned for him to peak in this second half of the race. None of it worried me. The way my legs felt that morning I was almost looking forward to it. Maybe Vincenzo Nibali would attack. Probably everyone would. Fine. Maybe not all of them had strolled to the bathroom that morning with the same easy energy as me.

On the bus on the way to the start, you could feel that same mix of tension and excitement that had been there on the morning of the Roubaix stage and the team time trial. It was there in the management, too. Nico Portal always asks Dave Brailsford if he'd like to add anything to the discussion he has just wrapped up perfectly well. Dave will usually begin by saying he has nothing to add, then talk in quite some detail for some time. This morning his words were all about what a great position we were in as a team, holding first and second place on the GC. Guys, it's the last day of a big block, let's keep this going. It was the other stuff that leaked in that told you how pumped he was. An edge to his voice. More gestures. Quite a bit more swearing.

Froomey cut through all the white noise. Guys, I want to attack on Alpe d'Huez today. When we get to five kilometres to the summit, I'm going to go. Okay?

Had I been on a rival team, listening in somehow, I would immediately have started plotting how to counteract his plans. The guy closest to you in the GC, only a minute and twenty-five seconds down, is going to attack you? Right. How can I mess things up for him?

Being teammates changed all that. If I chased Chris when he attacked, I'd simply tow all the other guys up to him. I'd damage both our chances. I'd let them chase him instead. I'd follow whoever was the strongest, let them do all the work. If they weren't closing and I felt like I could, I'd probably go a bit later.

Maybe I should have felt threatened. I had the lead, why wasn't I the leader? It was an easy answer for me. Because Froomey was the great champion. He had done it multiple times. The first week had long gone, when I had been a protected rider too. The decision to leave me had I punctured in the time trial, the fact that Chris had got the air con – these things were all gone. You ride for the team, and the team was in a fantastic position. He was allowed to say those things. Better too that he said it than didn't say it and did it anyway.

Away we went. God, it was hot. Maybe some of the spectators were treating the earlier climbs as a mere *hors d'oeuvre* for the famous finale to come, but they were big enough and nasty enough to crack you mentally long before Alpe d'Huez if you weren't feeling great. The heat would make everyone suffer, and surges in the pace would stretch us all out even more.

The 5,000m of climbing was too much to get your head around and feel okay about it. I broke what was coming into the three big climbs, and then broke those earlier climbs into chunks. The Madeleine and Croix de Fer were the longest climbs of the entire race. If you see the Madeleine as one long 25km slog, even if it's not super steep, the idea of it can crack you. The gradient on the Croix de Fer is not consistent. It goes steep climb, short descent, horrible steep, flattish section, steady climb, steep uphill again. I thought about each of them, because days like this were mental games as much as physical ones, or a nasty combination of the two. If you had doubts about your form before those climbs, then their length and relentless gradient would have the demons on your shoulder shouting and screaming. Everyone could ride at that early pace. It was nothing crazy hard. But with the heat, and the thought of the slogs to come, and Alpe d'Huez hanging over it all ...

All that to think about and you can forget to think about the simple stuff. It was a hot day, and early on I didn't drink enough. On a big day you've got to keep fuelling and keep drinking. I didn't, or at least not enough on the Madeleine, and the attacks were already swarming. Steven Kruijswijk, the Dutchman in the yellow and black jersey of LottoNL-Jumbo, had been lurking in sixth overnight, only two minutes and forty seconds down on me. When the early break went on that first climb, Kruijswijk got into it.

One thought: phew, that's a long way to go, let him go. Next one: but Luke and Gianni are already finding this pace hard. And I haven't drunk enough. And it's getting hotter with every half hour.

Okay. I haven't drunk enough, but I've seen the problem. If I sort it out now, I could still be okay. I haven't gone past the point of no return.

At the summit of the Madeleine, Kruijswijk was far enough up the road to be in the virtual yellow jersey. With 122km to go that didn't mean we had to panic. I drank hard on the blast up the Lacets and the approach to the Croix de Fer, and I started coming round again. I'd been wrapped up in my own little world of doubt for the first time all race. Not feeling good here, the other guys might be feeling a lot better ... Nah, come on, it's the lack of drink talking. Get your head straight. You're in yellow for a reason.

Kruijswijk was only just getting started. On that second big climb, he threw it all in. Warren Barguil is a quality climber but couldn't stay with him. Neither could Valverde. It takes close to an hour to conquer the Croix de Fer. By the top Kruijswijk had a lead of almost six minutes. An almost casual response flicking through the brain: 'Blimey, he's strong here ...'

Six minutes is the sort of gap that makes you ride hard in pursuit. We didn't panic – it wasn't ideal, but Wout was riding a decent tempo and keeping him at six minutes. Kruijswijk's advantage was more of a threat to the other teams, and so they eventually came to ride: Bahrain-Merida taking it on for Nibali and Movistar for Quintana and Landa. It should have made it easier having other teams share the workload, but that short surge each put in when they went to the front, even if only for a couple of minutes, became another test of belief and resolve. We had been riding for twelve days now, been out in France for more than two and a half weeks. When the pace cranked up I had to tell myself that this fresh pain was okay, that it was temporary, that it was no more than we could have thrown in. Anything else and it could have been the end. Start thinking about sitting up and you will sit up. Start believing that those others are stronger than you and you will ride as if it's true.

The team is more than the riders on the road. Having a sport director like Nico Portal came into its own once again when the pressure was on. Nico knows the Tour. He rode it six times in the first part of his career. He's young to be a DS, only seven years older than me, but his composure is that of a grizzled old man. Six minutes can spook you into doing daft things. Nico on the team radio was the voice of reason. 'Don't worry, guys, stay together. Okay, Kwiato, you're going to have to ride a bit earlier, but it's all okay.' The words were mollifying, even his voice calm.

There must have been immense stress on him. Dave sometimes messages him in the car during stages. For Nico to stay strong and do what he thinks is best when it's your boss challenging you takes courage. To keep that pressure from transmitting from him to us, to process all the information he's getting about where people are on the road, to think about the tactics, to do it all while driving one-handed ...

I listened to Nico, I held on and the pace dropped. Not firing bullets this time but biting one. I glanced at my Garmin. We were just holding the speed that Wout had been doing before.

Wout, however, was struggling. He'd ridden nearly the whole climb. After setting your own tempo for that long, a sudden surge is even harder on the head than the legs. He started to drift back. Then Bahrain and Movistar suddenly stopped riding. Ten minutes of work on the front and they'd already had enough. Okay, back to it, boys. Castro did the majority of the work, pushing his big Spanish engine into the red for us, and again as we swooped down into the valley for the flat twenty-kilometre stretch before Bourg d'Oisans and the hairpins beyond it. When he needed help, Kwiato stepped in earlier than planned. They rode again hard as we chased Kruijswijk's trace. Surely, I thought, he can't stay out there and hold all that lead, not into this headwind, on the flat, all on his own?

We picked up the scraps of the break left behind him – Barguil, Valverde, Pierre Rolland. Still no Kruijswijk. Tom Dumoulin with us, and Romain Bardet, as well as Landa after Movistar's work and Nibali profiting from Bahrain-Merida's efforts. There's no way he could pull this off, is there? Even if he gets close, he's still going to be working so much harder than us. Alpe d'Huez is a long climb to ride. It's well over forty minutes of eyeballs-out effort. It would be about this group, not his, no?

Into Bourg d'Oisans, the little town that lives because of the Alpe that towers overhead. The lead was four minutes and fifteen-ish seconds. The yellow jersey still heading his way if he could maintain that, still his if he could hang on and lose only a minute and a half on the climb, a bonus ten seconds there for winning the stage too.

Wout was gone. Kwiato gave it everything he had left on the first two kilometres out of the village, and then our crack Sky unit had become a trio: Froomey, the great champion; me, the race leader; and Egan Bernal, a skinny chap, a man with a huge future, suddenly being asked to deliver in the now to keep men a decade his senior alive on the most iconic climb of them all.

A word to Egan, who was a kid in the best sweetshop in cycling. Mate, you've got to take us to five kilometres from the top, okay? That's where Froomey wants to attack. I really don't want to have to ride.

Egan is a natural climber. Egan is a lad with rockets in his heels. Whoa, Egan, that's a great squeeze, but hold a little something back – that pace is amazing, but you've got to maintain this for six or seven kilometres and we've got to get to the finish twelve kilometres up the road. You're already showing us what you've got. No one's going to doubt you if you keep it a fraction steadier and work at the front for a little longer.

Nibali was the first to launch. Red jersey, gold detail, lean tanned legs. Me controlling Egan with as few words as possible. No worries. Hold. I didn't need 'squeeze'; he was already going.

Nibali soon back in the group. Quintana was the next. Same as before. The thought: this pace is red hot, if he takes twenty seconds here that'll cause so much damage he won't make it to see Froomey's attack, let alone the finish. Again nothing decisive, just a little jab from a distance, testing our reflexes. Were they serious attacks, or just to see what we had in our legs?

Bardet with a kick, to roars from the roadside. This was more serious, his body language more aggressive. Right, he means this. But still, he couldn't escape, not yet. The speed they attacked and the speed we were riding made it a sum they couldn't win. But there would be more.

I was suffering now. We were all suffering, but you can only feel your own pain. The others have it locked away behind their shades.

My head was pounding. That was the worst. The heat, up in the thirties, way beyond anything a kid from south Wales grows up riding in. I tried to focus on my breathing, to not let it get ragged.

It's the unknowns that torture you. Is everyone else feeling as bad as me? If I'm suffering, then they've got to be suffering as well, haven't they, after the day before? The pain so real, no longer just a mental block you can work your way around. Eight kilometres to go? Oh fuck. A surge of determination. I'm not going to get dropped at this pace. The kilometres will go. I'll feel all right.

Control. Deep breaths, control.

That settled me down a bit. I tried not to look at the kilometres, slowly ticking down, or the hairpins left to spin round. The odd glance at my Garmin to see the power I was putting out, to see if it felt this hard because we were riding hard. Cool. We are going fast. That's just the pace that is being set. Try to control the whole breathing, the out as well as the sucking in. Focus on that.

This moment in the race is almost the hardest. It's like the first 3,000m of a 4km team pursuit. It's hurting but still controlled, you just have to relax and take it. Riding at 90/95% is harder than just going all in. Stay strong. The legs are good, the head needs to be as well.

A roar from Cymru Corner as we came into view. Hairpin fourteen had never been particularly Welsh in the past, but now you couldn't miss the huge flags draped over the grey rock face. Nor could you miss the giant image of me in my Wales jersey, winning Commonwealth road gold in 2014. I knew my brother was there, I knew others had been trying to cycle up before the police cleared the roads.

Through Irish Corner, hairpin ten. Up to Dutch Corner, the original and best national invasion, a tribute to the early success of Dutch riders on Alpe d'Huez, to boozing in the open air, to the thrills of standing on a mountain when home is polder-flat. Everyone in orange, the techno blasting, every sort of fancy-dress as long as it was a certain colour. The last time we had ridden the corner, it had been insane, the hordes squeezing us into a single file of riders down a thin strip of clear road. This time the gendarmes had put ropes out to keep them back. Remarkably, the fans actually seemed to be staying behind them.

So many flares, so much smoke. There's an amazing

Right: You might not remember the 1997 British Schools Hill Climb Championships in Matlock. Twenty-one years later, I would be wearing the same colour jersey on the biggest stage of all.

Below: A decade on, and I can't quite believe I'm riding the prologue of the Tour de France, let alone that it's in the middle of London. The idea of winning the thing seemed as realistic as climbing Big Ben.

Above: This is the expression you make when you have just fractured your pelvis but don't realise yet. I still managed to finish the remaining 20 days of the 2013 Tour. Admittedly it did smart a little.

Left: 2015, and another Tour crash. This time it was Warren Barguil who smacked into me and sent me headfirst into a telegraph pole, and then down a ravine. Luckily I was fine – but I did lose my favourite Oakley sunglasses.

If ever a photo summed up the carnage of the cobbles it would be this one: Chris Froome going over Gianni Moscon; Alexander Kristoff and Greg van Avermaet trying not to go over Froomey.

The cobbled sectors on Stage 9: a world of dust and pain and your handlebars bouncing like a jackhammer. The race to get in the right position was even worse. Non-stop sprinting and stress. I sort of enjoyed it, once it was over.

Above: When you're in yellow you're a hunted man. But better to be the chased than the chasing.

Above left: Riding through the clouds, racing as I had always dreamed. With every day that passed I felt more in control. It was a surreal feeling.

Below left: The extra demands of wearing yellow. The daily ritual of questions.

Left: The Froomey Fist-Bump. He's not trying to be Jay-Z; we do it rather than shake hands for reasons of hygiene.

Right: Last-minute fine-tuning to my yellow skinsuit before the biggest day of my career. I'd watched Froomey do this in previous years. Now it was my turn.

Left: You never get tired of pulling on the yellow jersey. The more times I did it, the more superstitious I became. Sticking to the daily routine almost to the minute helped.

Rest day ride with the boys, France, July 2018.

The Champs-Elysees in Paris. Twenty-one stages and three weeks of racing behind us (plus photographer Russ Ellis).

Right: After the time-trial, the Tour won, doing it alongside one of the greatest. Forget the fist-bumps, now we could hug it out.

Left: Dave Brailsford and I get emotional after my Tour victory is sealed. "Don't start crying G, you'll set me off ..."

Right: The Tour de France is officially over, and I've won. Which makes this one of the best beers I've ever tasted.

At my homecoming parade in Cardiff. You never think about the aftermath of winning, just the actual winning itself. But to come home to thousands of my compatriots cheering me was something I'll never forget.

image that photographer Scott Mitchell took just after Dutch Corner, blue and yellow and red smoke thick around me, the sun behind giving it all a bit of a Renaissance painting feel, or at least a dirty nightclub where they've gone over the top with the dry ice and strobes. The yellow on my jersey and helmet picks out the yellow Pinarello lettering on my bike's down-tube, the white rims of my shades mirror the white backs of my gloves. My mouth open, right knee bent, left leg straightening as it pushes down hard. Spectators in the background all looking back down the road to see who's chasing and who's dropping.

You could proper feel the smoke going in your nose. It was horrible. But the whole insanity of the scene and atmosphere worked as the most tremendous accidental painkiller. I couldn't see any messages written on the road. We were over them too fast. But every flag overhead, every British voice in my ear, each banner I caught in my peripheral vision, was like a hand in the small of my back. You suffer alone on Alpe d'Huez but you keep going with the help of thousands of others.

Different parts of your body hurt at different times. The aches in your neck and the small of your back are earlier in the stage, when you've got time to think about those small details. If it's a steep climb and you've been out of the saddle a lot, your arms will be filling with lactic acid, a poison you've produced all on your own.

On Alpe d'Huez it was purely my legs and my breathing. Don't think about it, G, don't think about it.

I'd planned the technical stuff – when to take my last

caffeine gel, when to ditch my last bottle. There was a point where the fluid wouldn't have time to give me anything, but its weight would still hold me back. A full bottle weighs half a kilogram. I'd spent months obsessing over losing fractions of kilograms. Why carry something useless up a slope so steep most people would struggle to walk it without regular stops?

Egan at the front, Egan playing a blinder. We had known he was good; you don't win the Tour of California and Oro y Paz at that age, against those sorts of fields, unless you're something special. But we hadn't guessed he was going to be this good. Just when we needed it, when we had been stripped of all our more grizzled lieutenants, he was producing the ride of the day.

He had been chilled all race, getting an extra slice of Dave's attention each morning to keep him calm on the flat days, to not worry if he lost time there. The crash he had on the first day, the two at Roubaix – the one going straight through a corner, the other going straight into the back of the BMC car – could have messed with his head. We'd told him to get through the first week as best he could, to just stay in the line. Instead he always seemed to be at the back of the Sky bubble, which is the hardest place in the set-up to be. When rival riders saw Froomey and me going past on the train, they didn't care who was behind. They just piled in, and he was the one being chopped. But he grew up on mountain bikes. He has sharp elbows. He held the wheel really well, and now he was leading the charge too. Egan, the future might just be yours.

Bardet went again, a very Bardet thing to do. This time it was a proper assault, a hard kick and staying out of the saddle, jersey wide open to show the black strap of his heart-rate monitor against his pale bony chest, face shiny with perspiration. He took a gap and then he appeared to be holding it.

Egan rode, still knocking out a relentless tempo, until five kilometres arrived and then he was gone. Okay. I'll keep riding at this pace and then give a little spike as we come into the real manic part. The camper vans piled up along the verges, half the crowd with half their clothing off, the smoke and cans of beer being waved and as much fancy-dress as a Saturday afternoon at the cricket in Cardiff.

Kruijswijk's hard-earned advantage was floating away in the thin Alpine air – cut to two minutes after eleven of the twenty-one hairpins, down to forty seconds with four kilometres to go. My little spike of pace, and then Chris went, just as he had planned, though maybe a little later in the climb; then, just when the race was laid out as it should be – out of the saddle, his elbows out wide, Bardet sucked back to him.

No panic from me. I knew this was coming and I knew that the others would have to respond first. Nibali, Dumoulin, Landa, Roglič, all sat behind me, wondering which of the other poker players might crack first.

Nibali chased. He'd kept his powder dry across the first twelve days, which is classic Nibali. They call him the Shark of Messina. Like all sharks you never saw him until the moment he was ready to strike.

This time I never saw him until he was down on the road in front of me. I actually rode over his rear wheel, wobbled, took my foot out but stayed upright. I hadn't seen what he'd hit, only that the first person running over to help him was a fully grown man dressed as a red Smurf. Only later would we hear reports that a spectator had stepped out in front of him, camera to their face to take a headshot of their own, then ducked out of his path at the last moment and left the strap of their camera hanging out in the road. Nibali's handlebar snagged it. The guy instinctively hung on. Nibali went down.

The Smurf hauled him back to his feet and stuck him back on his bike. If that didn't freak Nibali out, then the pain of a fractured vertebra would have done. He would make it to the finish line but be forced to abandon there. First Richie Porte, now Nibali. Bad luck stalked you on every corner at the Tour de France.

Good luck can also appear on your shoulder. Dumoulin came past me as I began pedalling again. Tom's a time tri-aller. He rides mountains like he's chewing up a long effort on the flat – steady pace, working just within his limits, avoiding the sudden jumps in effort that push you into the red. He was going to try gradually hauling Froomey in, and that worked a treat for me. I stuck close to his back wheel and waited for the tow.

Chris had worked a lead of maybe 25m in that first 400m of his attack. In the same period, Kruijswijk's lead had been sliced to 20 seconds. That's how quickly fortunes change in the high mountains. Every margin is exaggerated, every advantage suddenly magnified. 200m later and Kruijswijk was toast. All that pain across all those kilometres, all that effort and hope and pain, and he had been caught with just over 2 miles of a 110-mile stage to go. The end is seldom dignified. You look back and you see the chaser and the legs that were so powerful just a few minutes before are suddenly dead. Kruijswijk lifted himself out of the saddle one more time, felt Froome on his wheel and pulled wide to let him through. Chris was past him like he was standing still.

When Chris is riding well his legs spin the pedals like clockwork toy. His head drops and moves from side to side as if he's spent but he never is. Except now, at the point where in his previous Tours he would be riding away, he was coming back to us. Tom had powered efficiently up to him, me on his wheel, Bardet on mine.

We were into the barriered section now, the crowds held back but the noise still thumping and distorting in your ears as if you were standing in front of the biggest speaker at a heaving festival. I had ditched that final bottle, unzipped my yellow jersey all the way down. Three kilometres to go, four of us in a thin line above the clouds.

Another little effort from Chris. Sat on Dumoulin, I could tell two things: that Tom was strong, and that Froomey wasn't as he had been twelve months before, or on Mont Ventoux in 2016, or in the mountains in 2015. There wasn't quite the same punch. Okay. Reassessment of tactics. Tom is the strongest, I'll just sit on him.

Bardet had another dart, realised it had failed and pulled over. And so, like exhausted boxers leaning on the ropes, we all sat back and drifted for a moment and found ourselves riding four abreast, like a group of old mates enjoying a Sunday spin along a local country lane, rather than a quartet of the best cyclists in the world in the last critical stretch of the most famous road in the sport.

A drop in speed, an acceleration for the senses. No longer trying not to think about the kilometres left, I'm telling myself not to let anyone get away now, to follow Tom, that this could come down to a sprint at the end.

With 2.5km to go, it hit me for the first time: I might actually be racing for the stage here. Just as I hadn't thought in advance about winning at La Rosière, there had never been a moment all day when I considered the possibility of winning on Alpe d'Huez. It was only stay with Dumoulin and Nibali and Froome. Don't lose time, don't lose touch.

Four of us, spread out, Landa coming back to us and Nibali closing again too. Part of me thinking, we should ride together now and at least keep Landa and Quintana and the other stragglers off. Another part responding, yeah, but it's the other guys who should be more concerned about doing that than me. I'll stay in and play their game.

2.4km. Bardet once more, throwing his bike from side to side, his jersey wide open and trailing in the wind. The crowds going ballistic, yells for him, some boos for the two Brits in behind. Froome trying to jump across, me coupled up again to the Dumoulin engine.

2.2km. Dumoulin no longer following but going himself. No more stop-start. A race once more. No more time trialling, now kicking like a pure climber. On his wheel, spotting it, staying on his wheel, covering it. Chris not with us, Bardet not with us.

On to a stiff 11% ramp. Tom not pulling away, the chasing two out of the saddle and firing bullets in every direction to get back on. 1.8km, all back together.

Into the ski resort itself, shifting suddenly from bright sunshine and noise into a tunnel, all darkness and silence except for the echoes of our breath. Tom still leading, then me, then Chris, then Bardet. 500m of riding, all of us mouths hanging open, sucking in the air, glancing around to see who might twitch next.

People hanging off the balconies of the chalets either side of the road. Spectators four deep along the barriers, leaning over, waving fists and flags. Landa back with us, yellow helmet, pale blue jersey.

Under the *flamme rouge*. 1,000m to go.

900, 800. 5 hours and 18 minutes of racing, all of it coming down to the next 60 seconds.

700m to go, and Landa launched from the back. The surprise attack, coming from the rear, the last man to arrive at the party and the first to leave.

I was on him, quicker than Tom, quicker than Froomey. Round a right-hander, dipping right again off a roundabout, a quick glance behind to see who was where.

400m, a slight curve left, 300, a steeper left, Landa hugging the inside of the bend. A look over my right shoulder and then swinging out wide so I could cut the apex and keep all that precious speed. Why was no one else taking it wide?

Kicking hard hard hard out of the bend. No more Landa

in my vision, just open road climbing up towards a red arch. So much in my legs suddenly, all that suffering banished and gone.

I might have this. Where are the others?

In that initial five-second acceleration out of the corner, I felt as I do when sprinting in training, all fresh and hungry. Like Sir Chris Hoy almost at the end of three laps of a 250m velodrome, gripping the bars and solid through my arms and shoulders and core, all that strength surging through my legs. Getting hold of the bike and letting it flow underneath me. Feeling the speed, the wind on my face, the power going through the pedals.

I had a little look under my arms and I couldn't see anyone. Don't look back properly now, got to keep going full on for the line, as soon as you look back you're going to slow down a bit.

Dropping back into my saddle, knowing that after all that team pursuit training on the boards, for all those years, that my seated power is just as good as when I'm up sometimes. One hundred metres. Back out again, head down, staying low against the barrier of air.

Thirty metres. Twenty metres. Ten.

It all hit me five metres before the line. Shit, I'm about to win Alpe d'Huez.

Through the line, throwing myself upright, mouth open, roaring. Elbows in my side, palms up, fists clenched. It's not a classic cycling celebration, arms straight out to the side, but I haven't won stages regularly enough to quite know what to do. I'm not Cav. You can see my love of rugby and football in it, plus a little bit more bicep, which is no bad thing for a cyclist's puny arms. The smile could come later. The happiness was exploding out of me but I am, after all, a British male.

A squeeze of the brakes, trying to catch my breath. Unclipping from the pedals, lifting my head to see my soigneur. A sweaty, shouty bear hug. Seeing someone I knew brought reality into the impossible. Man, I just won Alpe d'Huez!

I'd watched this mountain and its heroes for so long over the years. Never did I think it would be possible for me. And here I was, cameras in my face, microphones and excited faces, the first Briton ever to win on the Alpe, the first man in the yellow jersey to win a stage up here.

Brad had been the first Brit to win the Tour. Froomey had been the first Brit to win the Giro. All the firsts were going. And I'd bagged a couple of cool ones that were just as unfeasible two days before. Phew, it's me doing it . . .

All those clichés about Alpe d'Huez, that it's cycling's Wembley, Lord's, St Andrews. I felt like I'd scored a try for Wales at the Principality Stadium – no, in some foreign field, in the World Cup final, All Blacks players lying broken on the turf behind me. I could think of nothing bigger than winning here, in yellow, at the Tour.

It wasn't a breakaway that the better riders had let go. It wasn't a late escape that had no effect on the GC. It was the best riders in the race, repeatedly attacking each other, everyone going for it, everyone on the limit. I barely even considered what it meant for my chances of staying in yellow, the ten-second bonus for winning the stage plus the two-second gap on the line meaning I was now a minute and thirty-nine seconds up over Froome and a minute fifty over Dumoulin. I was deep in the moment, deep in the pure thrill of it all.

I spotted George, the Team Sky press officer. George is a calm man, naturally laid back. Not in this moment. 'G, what the hell's just happened?'

Seeing the win reflected on familiar faces added authenticity to the weirdness of it all. A lot were trying to do what I usually do and not get carried away, talking about how there was still so far to go in the race, not to think beyond tomorrow, even as the desire to jump around was clearly visible too. I didn't see Dave until we got back to the bus. Dave is a natural hugger, in a grab-you-and-squeeze sort of way. 'Wow, fucking hell, G! Well done!' Rod's reaction was a joy. Someone who cares about you letting the world know how much.

In the press conferences afterwards the giddiness was still with me. 'I don't know what to say. This is unbelievable. Can we just go straight to Paris now? After today, I can be happy.'

So too was the default settling. The leadership of the team, G. Is that yours now or Chris's?

'This race is so hard and you never know how the body reacts. I'm still riding for Froome. He's still the man. He won it four times and is probably the best ever. I'm just going to enjoy this.'

I floated back to my hotel room, lay down on the bed and called Sara. It was the first stage she had been able to bring herself to watch and our conversation was even more British than my celebrations on the line had been.

'Alright?'

'Yeah, you?'

'Yeah, that was alright, wasn't it?'

'Yeah, not too bad ... Bloody hell, you just won Alpe d'Huez!'

'Ha ha, yeah! You have a good day?'

Sara Thomas

I think if I lost faith then Geraint would lose faith. You need to draw from each other. If I say it's going to be fine and I sound like I really believe it, he kind of convinces himself. 'I'm going to be fine, I am not cursed.' I believe because you believe.

I don't want to be nervous around him. I keep it all in. I don't want to talk about it when people ask. I can't forget about it, but whatever happens, I'll deal with it.

On the La Rosière stage I was staying with my brother and his wife, not wanting to watch for fear of what might happen. My phone started pinging. Right, it's either really good or really bad. I had been chatting all race with Fran Millar, and our tactic, our little keep-calm joke, had been to repeat certain phrases to each other: it's all normal, it's just another race, it's fine.

Fran's text arrived. 'This is completely normal.' Oh. This has got to be good then. I looked at my phone. Bloody hell, he's won ...

You'd think people would start jumping up and down, but you don't. You're so happy, but you're also aware that they've got to do it all again the next day, that it changes in an instant. That it's Geraint. I am so used to it going wrong. But the bad times have also taught us to celebrate the good, so we always will. I'll have a glass of bubbly but I won't let myself get carried away. I'll enjoy the moment, but cork the feeling and celebrate properly at the end, when everything's done and he's back safe and sound.

I forced myself to watch Alpe d'Huez. When Ger went on the front for Froomey, I thought, okay, that's it, he can't be feeling that great, he'd only do that now if he thought he was going to be dropped. That's it, it was nice while it lasted. Then the Nibali crash happened and I couldn't see Geraint at all. So. Either he's blown spectacularly in the last ten seconds and he's at the back, or he's on the floor. At that point I didn't know what was best.

All of the sudden this yellow jersey appears. You get a surge of pure joy. Then you feel a surge of guilt, because you know Nibali's partner is watching at home thinking, oh shit, it's him. And I've been there so many times, you're so relieved that it's not your man.

I'm an awful watcher. I can't speak. Yet when he crossed the finish line, all of a sudden I was shouting. 'Come on, Geraint!' Not really jumping up and down, more in shock. I can't believe that's just happened . . .

I'd built myself up for it not going to plan. I thought he'd gone. I thought he was working for Chris. I thought he was going to be dropped. I'd come to terms with, okay, he's had the jersey for a day, that was cool, now normal service has been resumed. Then this happened. Bloody hell! Seeing it all on television made me want to be there and experience it all. Not miles away, sat there feeling sick.

If I hadn't experienced the lows, I probably would have got a lot more excited. I'd been left scarred from races past. Looking back, I wish I'd been able to enjoy it more, to let myself get carried away and soak it all in. But I couldn't shake the feeling that something, at some point, was going to go wrong.

I'm normally a positive person, but a part of me was just waiting for something bad to happen, rehearsing what I was going to say to him this time when it did. I knew that whatever happened now we had a lot to celebrate in Paris, but I couldn't let myself get carried away, in fear that the thought alone of him winning was enough to jinx the whole thing. Such a mix of emotions, so much happiness but also the realisation that there was still such a long way to go. If he was just plodding along quite nicely it would be easier to come to terms with it if something happened. But the better he was doing and the further we got into it, the harder it got to watch, because you think there's so much more to lose now.

It doesn't get easier. It gets worse.

Chapter Eleven

Keeping the Pain at Bay

The Tour only looks forward, at least until it's done. Yesterday's winner will never be forgotten, but the next day he's just another one of the 165-ish tired riders left in a race that charges on, and on, and on.

You win a one-day race in northern Europe and all night it's ten per cent Belgian beers brewed by monks with too foamy a head and possibly an unnecessary fruit-based flavouring component. Win a Tour stage, you do more interviews and you enjoy a few sips of champagne, but there's no lie-in, no treat pizzas or rehydrating on something that is guaranteed to give you a headache as well as a good time. Win two stages in a row and there are even more interviews, and still no rest. The Tour never looks back.

The time would come. Every winner of a Tour stage that finishes on Alpe d'Huez gets a named plaque on one of the hairpins. Mine would be corner fifteen, a nice left-hander. As a pro cyclist, you are forbidden from going skiing. Too dangerous for our precious legs. I had always loved the idea of going the first winter after my retirement. Now I had a new layer on that ambition: go back and stay at the summit resort with the kids I hope to have one day, ski down and slide to a halt. 'Hey, Thomas juniors. Look up there. See that plaque?' 'Whatever, Dad. Beat you to the bottom. When did you get so fat?'

Age teaches you to squeeze every drop of enjoyment you can out of a win. When I first won Olympic gold in Beijing, I was so blinkered that all I could think about was the final and nothing else. Four years later in London, I wanted to take in every single nuance. I realised how lucky I was to be a British athlete experiencing a home Olympics. When we were at our team holding camp in Newport, when we were in the Olympic village in Stratford, I watched every television preview programme and as many events during it as I could. My roommate Ed Clancy couldn't understand it. He wanted to pretend none of it was happening. 'Turn that off, G. Put anything else on. It's making me nervous . . .'

I was like that the morning after the Alpe d'Huez/La Rosière summit double. I wanted to settle down and relive it again, to watch it back on television in real time. Not in a self-indulgent way, to see how wonderful I'd been, but because it had been so much fun. You know the day after your wedding when you really want to see all the photos your mates have taken? It was like that. I didn't want to stick my suit and tie on again and go to another wedding while I was still buzzing off mine.

I tried to use the warm memories to keep me going forward, too. It had already been a special two weeks. If it were to end tomorrow, I wanted to enjoy it now and remember all it had been. I also understood how much better yet it could be. Stay focused, G, do everything right. The stuff that's done will still be there in ten days' time for you to relish. See what other beautiful memories it might be possible to create.

Sara was feeling the pressure. In that perverse way that sport works, the better it was going for me the more nervous she was becoming, because there was so much more to lose. For me, because I was the one doing it, it was the opposite. I was feeling great. I had no premonitions that I might crack. With every mountain stage that came and went, I was becoming more confident.

The Tour always marches on but it has its natural lulls too. Stage 13 could not have been better designed for men heavy-legged after three days in the mountains. It started at the bottom of the Alpe at Bourg d'Oisans and then travelled pretty much downhill all the way to Valence, 169.5km away, through Grenoble and arcing north towards Voiron before heading south-west once again. It was a finish to suit the sprinters and a day to please those keen to freewheel; we would begin at 700m above sea level and end it at 153m.

The whole peloton was looking for an easy day, and we got it, probably the easiest of the entire Tour. None of us wanted a punchy break to go away, no one wanted to be chasing full gas. Thomas De Gendt kicked one off, because that's what he does, and Dimitri Claeys, Tom Scully and Michael Schär went with him, but none of those were con-tenders on the GC, and the sprinters' teams kindly did all the work at the front of the bunch – Groupama-FDJ, UAE Team Emirates and Bora-Hansgrohe.

The Alps had done a brutal job on the fast men. As well as Mark Cavendish, Marcel Kittel and André Greipel, Fernando Gaviria and Dylan Groenewegen had all missed time-cuts and were gone from the race. That lack of contenders can actually make a sprint stage messier. Suddenly you get guys who are second or third tier sprinters now believing they've got a chance. Their team wants to help them, but they don't necessarily know how to do it properly. Cav or Gaviria, there's that mutual respect, and you give them a bit of room and let them go. The others? You're not confident they'll end up where they should. But you could tell that day that everyone was reeling from the big block of racing from Roubaix through all those big mountain days, and so we chilled, if you can chill at 42kph with your front wheel three inches from the back wheel of the man in front. The final fifteen kilometres got stressful, because they always do, but the roads were wide and fast, and there was no headwind, and we could all watch Peter Sagan go away and strut his stuff to take the stage win from Alexander Kristoff and Arnaud Démare after Philippe Gilbert launched late and long in a very Philippe Gilbert way.

Sagan summed it up nicely afterwards: 'This stage was a piece of gold for us.' A collective sigh of relief that the Alps were behind us for another year, a subtle fist-pump from me that I had gained time on all my rivals on two of the three days and only not done so on the other because the team didn't have to. My lead was good, and that made my position a lovely one. I didn't have to take any risks. Keep the bullets on my bandolier. If I could nick a second or two then I'd go for it, but otherwise let the others roll the dice.

This was my mantra throughout these three days in the deep south, working our way from Alps to Pyrenees through the Ardèche and onwards south-west. The challenge on Saturday, 21 July came not from the wooded valleys and secret rivers we would skirt from Saint-Paul-Trois-Châteaux to Mende, but the climb that came at the death. The Tour has finished a few times in Mende, and when it does, we always end on a local airstrip that is on top of a plateau above the town, accessible only via a horrible road called the Côte de la Croix Neuve. It was just over three kilometres long, but it went straight up in the air – an average gradient of more than 10%, ramps on its journey of 18%.

It always seemed to produce dramatic finishes. Local hero Laurent Jalabert had won there in 1995, when it made its Tour debut, and some still called it his mountain. Then Steve Cummings, my good mate and ex-teammate, had pulled off a sweet heist there in 2015 as Romain Bardet and Thibault Pinot went all dithery in the final flat kilometre at the top.

I say Sa had been nervous and I had been fine, but I was pretty squeaky on the long transition to Mende. It was such a punchy climb that I wondered if it would suit Froomey more than me. Dumoulin I thought I could take up there because it was so steep, but maybe its shortness played into his hands. Would Primož Roglič have a pop, or Bardet try to make up for his missed opportunity three years before?

Once again those of us tilting at the GC let a big harmless break go away. It effectively made the day one of two races:

the one for the stage win, which Omar Fraile would nab from Jasper Stuyven after battling past him on the steepest part of the final climb, and the one for the positions inside the overall classification, some eighteen minutes back.

Luke Rowe positioned us a treat coming into Mende's ancient streets. AG2R were trying to do a similar job for Bardet. The climb jumped up at you and so – more noticeably than on some of the set-piece Alpine climbs – did a few spectators too.

I was riding hard, watching Egan Bernal's rear wheel, twitchy for the attacks from behind that would surely come. When I'm pushing that much, I don't take in much of what else might be around me. But on the hillside the hostility was fierce and it was unavoidable.

The Côte de la Croix Neuve is not a big, wide road designed for mass tourism, like Alpe d'Huez. People don't come in their thousands throughout the year to pay homage – which is probably just as well, because there was no room for camper vans and Dutch invasions. There was a steep, wooded slope on one side, a narrow verge and precipitous drop the other. A long wait for us to arrive, a fair amount of booze taken on board, a fair amount of boos the result.

Everything about it felt different. Claustrophobic where the Alps had been big views and clear peaks. Darker green, more rain that summer there than the sun-bleached pastures back east. Fewer fans from across the world, more from the Massif Central.

It wasn't just we Sky boys who noticed it. Luke Durbridge, the Aussie riding for Mitchelton-Scott, tweeted about it afterwards. 'What I sore from the fans on the final climb today towards @TeamSky was disgraceful. We are all human and we are all suffering regardless what jerseys we have on. If you don't like cycling don't come to watch!!'

Forgive him the grammatical error. Sore gets on your mind two weeks into a Tour. He took so much abuse for that tweet, but he knew what he saw and heard. Froome had some sort of liquid flicked at him from a bottle. Maybe it was water. I hope so.

In the moment, in the race. The pain was at bay today, the gradient steep but melting away under my wheels. Roglič went. We held him, and held him. Dumoulin dropped, found his mojo and ground his way back on. Froomey stayed with us, but it took what seemed like a substantial effort. Egan Bernal was our front marker again, but I kept finding myself riding alongside him, thinking, are you going to go a bit quicker then, what are you waiting for? Dumoulin attacked, I responded. I was genuinely surprised when I looked back and it was only Froomey behind, no Quintana, Landa, Bardet and Kruijswijk. Confidence surged as a result. Wow. I'm feeling so good here . . .

I could cover every move. I'd managed the same at the Dauphiné; maybe I should have been used to it. But in my head, if I was ever going to win a Grand Tour, it was going to be like when I won Paris–Nice. It would come down to the wire, barely a handful of seconds in it, desperately chasing down a descent somewhere to hold on. What was this?

Roglič held on to a scrawny lead as we came over the top and finished down the airstrip. Eight seconds taken, for all that effort, but no serious advance on me at the top of the leaderboard. Quintana lost ten seconds on me, Chris and Tom. Bardet fourteen, Mikel Landa twenty-nine. There were patterns emerging here. There were patterns becoming almost predictable.

So were the smattering of boos when I was being zipped into another fresh yellow jersey on the podium. I told the media afterwards that I'd rather hear jeers on the top step than cheers on the back seat of the bus. Nor did I think they were specific to me; it was more of a generic Sky thing, some of it from the team's dominance of a French race, some of it from what felt like a misrepresentation of Chris's now-closed salbutamol case. Back in 2014, when Chris had crashed out and we couldn't win a stage, the booing had gone. We were loved for trying and failing. When we were winning again the following year all the heckling came back.

I honestly didn't feel we were winning in a boring way. Maybe I'm looking at it through rose-tinted glasses, but Alpe d'Huez had been the best race up there in years. It was insane. And La Rosière's multiple plot-lines kept us all guessing until the final 200m. But a minority appeared only to recognise or appreciate panache when it ended in failure. Football crowds don't cheer a winger who beats two men and then falls over by the corner flat. If I'm at Twickenham and a Welsh prop sets off on a run from under his own posts, steps a defender and then loses the ball in the tackle on his own twenty-two-yard line, I don't purr with admiration. Was trying to win and succeeding not the basic principle of professional sport? Maybe we needed to pull more comedy faces at the television motorbikes. That always seemed to tickle some locals.

The verbal abuse I was fine with. If you're an Arsenal player going to Spurs, you're going to get it in the ear for the full ninety minutes, get called all sorts of things. If anyone threw a coin, however, or tried to slap a player, they'd be gone. There are also hundreds of stewards in place keeping an eye on the wilder elements of the crowd.

Chris had been clouted by a fan on Alpe d'Huez and had something thrown at him today. In a few days' time I would be grabbed at on another steep climb and almost brought down. We would cycle more than 3,300km in this Tour, and three or four incidents spread out over that distance was a minuscule proportion, but after thirteen days of abuse, we wondered if everything was being done that could be. Of course putting barriers along every metre of the route was an impossibility – and the guy who tried to impede me was behind barriers anyway – but attacks like these didn't happen in Spain, at the Vuelta. Alberto Contador had actually served a doping ban and got a hero's reception everywhere he rode. Even at the Giro, where Chris had one spectator run alongside him dressed as an asthma inhaler – you had to give the bloke credit for his costume – the racing was uninterrupted.

You could feel it growing, almost without conscious thought, like when you're queuing at the airport and one person ducks under the tape to cut the line and suddenly everyone's following him. There was a mob mentality in a few places, and you could sense it spreading up certain climbs. I wouldn't say it worried me, but it was certainly on my mind. Would we have to ride in the middle of the road at all times in case one rogue idiot decided to ruin it for everyone else? The race needed protecting, not just for Sky but for everyone watching.

Still. I was also discovering the pleasurable, small perks that came with being in yellow. Not for the race leader a remount and ride back down the climb they've just come up, or an hour of frustration stuck in the vast cavalcade of cars and buses and trucks trying to get back down the same narrow roads. Instead, a seat in the podium car, with Froomey's bodyguard at the wheel. And Froomey's body-guard can really drive – he was flying down, with millimetres either side, always in total control; our team doctor in front was going green at the gills but press officer George and I were in awe of his skills. It must have saved us an hour at least. It was like being cycling royalty. I could get used to this, I thought.

Sunday, 22 July. Stage 15, from Millau to Carcassonne. 181.5km south towards the Spanish border and the Pyren-ees, sliding past Castres. Real rugby union territory, which brought a warm glow to this Welshman's heart.

In the same way that the Côte de la Croix Neuve had been the spectre at the Mende feast, the bump in today's Sunday menu was the Pic de Nore. It wasn't huge – 12.3km at an average of 6.3% – but it had something of a local reputation. A mini Mont Ventoux, some called it, because the dense vegetation on its lower slopes gave way to bare rock and thin pasture towards the top, and a tall radio mast dominated the summit. You could argue that a mini Ventoux wasn't really a Ventoux at all, in the same way that you couldn't have a mini Massif Central. The climb was hard enough to cause damage in the peloton; if the stage finished up there, the GC would certainly be affected. But with a 20km descent followed by 20km of flat, nobody was going to go away and then hold their advantage to the finish. Maybe if there were four or five guys, but if four or five guys went you wouldn't give them anywhere near as much rope as someone going solo.

With a week to go until we finished in Paris, and a rest day on the Monday before we returned to the big steep stuff in the Pyrenees, people were wondering where I might crack, where the classic G bad day would come. I was feeling remarkably calm. There was some soreness in the legs from Mende's examination, but tiredness is a relative concept on the Tour. I was almost embarrassed to realise that everyone else seemed even more tired. Some of them were screaming. Confidence came from those little jolts of dominance: from looking back on the final climb above Mende on Saturday and seeing nobody with us; from Dumoulin only really having that one strong pace rather than a Quintana ability to go hard, get a substantial gap, recover and go hard again; Froomey having a little dig but not being able to break us, Froomey later not really being able to give me a turn on the front so we could gap Tom.

All those sensations were there, feeling good, hoping for

more. I let them bubble without boiling over into overconfidence or recklessness; I kept a lid on them. I reminded myself not to do anything too crazy, just keep going like this.

I'm not someone who outwardly looks super-excited about things. It's there inside, but I keep it locked up. That morning I found it easier than in years before. Some of the races where I'd got close in the past, like Paris–Nice in 2016, I hadn't really been able to sleep much the night before the final stage. The first time you do anything, your brain's not accustomed to it and goes on red alert. But I'd now won big stage races a few times, and I'd been in yellow at these last two Tours for a cumulative week. So as the days went on, it was becoming easier and easier to stay calm. Had I been struggling physically, the fear would have been nudging me every time I was alone. Whoa, I could lose this at any point . . . Instead it seemed very simple. Enjoy it. Keep doing what I'm doing. Eat and drink the correct things at the right times. If I'm going to blow I'm going to blow. It was a very logical approach to what could be a highly emotional outcome, but why overthink it? If I've done all I can and someone still drops me or I have a bad day, then so be it. For now, I'm feeling good and riding well. It made more sense that I should keep feeling good and riding well than the opposite to suddenly happen.

A Sunday where someone would win, a day I only had to not lose. The break went away after about forty kilometres. Great. I sat in the middle of the white-shirted Sky bubble. Perfect. The Pic de Nore rose up in front of us and immediately felt familiar. With its dark trees giving way to bushes and heather and open fields, it could have been the Rhigos in south Wales or a climb from the Tour of Britain on Dartmoor or in the Yorkshire Dales. It wasn't too long and it wasn't too steep. Rafał Majka attacked from the breakaway; Magnus Cort and Bauke Mollema chased him. Noises in the distance, rumblings from a different war.

This idea that Sky race negatively: we ride in the manner that will best help us win. We had won five of the previous six Tours and three Grand Tours in succession. After that it's hard to care if people see it as boring or not. The Pic de Nore and its descent showcased an alternative approach, and it was not an alluring one. The French rider Julien Bernard had a solo go on the lower slopes. He's a nice guy, Julien, and he's got pedigree: his dad, Jean-François, was part of Bernard Hinault's team at La Vie Claire in the 1980s. He came third at the 1987 Tour and won a stage up the actual Ventoux. But it was a doomed move. It was never going to work. Neither was Dan Martin's lonely attack, not with forty kilometres to go. Dan's a mate. He's super-strong on climbs. I'm sure he was hoping that someone else would jump out to him, although he said afterwards that he was just bored and that riding doesn't hurt if you're having fun. But it's still a race and everyone still wants to crack you as a team, and I'm guessing that's what he was trying to do. To me he was wasting bullets in a fight he could never win. Why not use them when you could actually hit something, rather than firing them into the sky?

On the descent it was Bardet's turn to throw logic out of the window. Full gas down the first three kilometres, at a point in the stage where he was never going to work a worthwhile advantage. Stress for him, stress for everyone now strung out behind. On one corner the inevitable happened: he went too hard into a hairpin, almost lost his back wheel and came within centimetres of disappearing off the side of the road.

This surge of speed for a few kilometres meant the minute and a half advantage Dan had over the top was down to less than thirty. We soon caught it. Finally Bardet settled down. I came alongside him. 'What are you doing? There's at least thirty-eight kilometres to go and fifteen or twenty of them are flat with a little crosswind. What are you risking all this for?'

He didn't reply. He doesn't tend to. He hadn't in the Dauphiné, when I had punctured and his team had appeared to attack as a direct result. Maybe he doesn't understand the Cardiff accent. But the unnecessary stress was back as we approached the ninety-degree right-hand corner which turned into a crosswind section that took us pretty much to the finish. It wasn't crazy strong, but was enough to make everyone tense.

A tiny amount of crosswind, a load of lightweight climbers trying to set up echelons, the work of the big strong rouleurs. Peter Sagan is quite loud in the bunch, you always know where he is. A shout in his strange Slovakian English, much weirder than the Cardiff drawl. 'Hey guys! What are we doing? There's no wind!'

If avoiding that stress and those spendthrift moves was negative, then we were negative. But we were through to the finish once again without major scares, with me still in yellow and Chris in second place. Thirteen minutes up the road, Magnus Cort had won the battle within the breakaway. Let him enjoy being the centre of the drama for the day.

What good does stress ever do you? You're stuck in traffic. Do you have a hover-car? Unfortunately not. Just relax, then. You're late for a flight. You miss the flight. You get another flight. It's a waste of money but it's not the end of the world.

I've always had that in me, and the work I did with Steve Peters as part of the GB team pursuit squad tightened it further. Steve, clinical psychiatrist, mind guru to the stars of British cycling, used to talk of the illogical side of your brain as a chimp. At your moments of maximum stress, the chimp starts screaming in your ear. You can't do this, you're going to fail, think of all the things that could go wrong. What if, what if, what if . . .

Steve reinforced what I was already doing. Stay logical. Stay in control. Believe in what you can do and are doing and have been for ages.

I took a lot from my time on the track: power, speed, discipline. But nothing was more important than the mental strength. I had been part of a quartet that went into a home Olympics as overwhelming favourites for gold. You could never again recreate that expectation and pressure. In the velodrome in Stratford there had been a Big Ben-style chime, counting down the seconds as you got on your bike. It was a lovely idea for the spectators but the worst thing you could possibly imagine for the riders. The intensity around you as you walked from the waiting area to your bike, as you raced in that bedlam – four years and so much relentless hard work, all of it coming down to those ten minutes on an August evening. Leading the Tour was big, but the demands on me were of a different magnitude. This was about hope rather than certainty. It was about could be rather than had to be.

There were riders alongside me as we rolled into Carcassonne for whom the Tour was everything. It mattered more than their personal lives and their partners. I was desperate to hang on to yellow if I could. I would be devastated if it went tits up now, to be going so well yet to lose it. I also knew it was just a bike race. If I won, my life would change a great deal. But my life was also pretty good before we had even begun a fortnight ago.

A nice moment as we came through the finish from one of the Sunweb riders. 'Hey man, I really hope you win the Tour. It would be great for you but also the sport, man . . .' It was the first time I'd heard that, and from a rider in a rival team it felt genuinely cool. It was also the first time someone had talked to me about winning the Tour. Journalists did but that was different. They were asking the question and I wasn't willing to comprehend it. From a rider it felt real.

And I never once found myself wishing it were over. There had been races before when I had been riding to the start line on a big day and thought, phew, it would be nice to be a helper rather than a leader today and be able to swing off at the bottom of the climb, no pressure, just ride to the finish. This time, I didn't have that thought once. I was genuinely enjoying it.

If you can be a professional elite sports person and get the same pleasure from it as you did as a kid, it's just playing for you. And who gets stressed just playing?

Chapter Twelve

Me v. Him

You're meant to relish your rest days as a rider at the Tour de France. Sleep. Get massaged. Do that little rest-ish ride, and then sleep some more.

I'd have been quite happy if Monday, 23 July hadn't happened at all. It wasn't just the hotel we had been allotted in Carcassonne, which was nowhere near the famous old medieval castle that everyone comes to see and very close instead to the dual carriageway junction where everyone who comes to see the famous old medieval castle turns off. It was that I didn't want to stop.

Why would I? We were on such a roll – the team, our tactics, our positioning on the road and on the general classification. I had been desperate to see Sara for weeks, and suddenly she was there with me and it threw me completely. Sharing a small room with someone, having their bags where your bags go, having another washbag in the bathroom, yours no longer where you're used to it being. Then there was how real leading the Tour now felt when I had the person I care about more than anyone else, who cares about me more than anyone else, right there with me.

I was on edge. Usually everyone's partners came out on the rest day, but this time there was only Egan's girlfriend and

Castro's wife and kids. Nobody normally cared what couples did on those days at the team hotel – we could walk around as we pleased, use the front door, go out for dinner – because the attention was always on Froomey or Dave. But all of a sudden Sa and I were having to sneak out the back to get some food because I was being mobbed. I hated walking past people who were asking for my autograph because as soon as you stop for one, you need to do them all; you can't leave a few hanging and wondering why they're the unlucky ones. So fire escapes it was, and a cap pulled low over my face, and anonymous clothes rather than anything with prominent Sky logos all over it. Or yellow.

I was glad Sa was there but I also wanted to stay in my happy zone. I had a morning routine and I found comfort in that routine. I didn't want to change anything that had worked so well over the past sixteen days, and I was starting to become more superstitious, or at least more superstitious about being superstitious.

We have a suitcase and we have what we call a dead bag, which stays on the team truck rather than the coach. Stick stuff in the dead bag that you don't need again until Paris. The suitcase was becoming heavy with yellow jerseys – you get a new one on the podium every day you hold the lead – as well as cuddly toy lions, which you also receive on a daily basis. Right, I thought – I'll stick the jerseys in the dead bag. Actually, maybe I should keep them in my suitcase. I could chuck a load of other spare clothes in there instead. So I did, and then had immediate second thoughts. Hang on, maybe I shouldn't change anything . . .

Come on, G, you're a logical man. You survived the London Olympics and Ed Clancy's fear of the Unknown Curse. You've shone under Steve Peters. If you get dropped on the way to Bagnères-de-Luchon tomorrow it's not going to be because you put a winter jacket from your suitcase into the dead bag. I had attached the lucky little silver wishbone that Sa had given me to the Garmin on my handlebar stem. I wasn't worried about losing it: for Tim Kerrison, those Garmins – containing all our data from every single day's ride – are like children. He wouldn't misplace them.

No one wanted to talk to me about the possibility of me winning it, in case it somehow put the mockers on it. So instead it all poured out to Sa when I wasn't listening. George had a word with her. 'Do you think he's going to win?' Another one of the staff tried tiptoeing round the issue. 'He's doing well, isn't he?' Sa and I certainly couldn't discuss it. It was a giant yellow elephant in the room. Let's just be normal. Yeah, but this isn't normal. At all.

The juxtaposition led to a few fraught moments. Our team doctor gives us small pots each day to urinate into so he can check our hydration levels and see how our health is. I had left mine, as always, on the cistern of the bathroom toilet. Sa, reaching for the flush, accidentally knocked the pot into the bowl as the water swirled around.

All I heard was the flush going and then Sa came out with her hand over her mouth. 'Ger, I'm sorry. Your wee-pot's gone in the toilet.'

It doesn't take much to set you off when you're leading

the Tour and feeling weird because you're not actually on your bike.

'WHY DID YOU FLUSH IT?'

'I didn't . . .'

'I HEARD IT!'

We got round it. Sa fished the pot out and rinsed it under the tap. I ended up getting a new one from the doctor just in case. But it encapsulated the weirdness of husband and wife being together in entirely unfamiliar circumstances. She was almost glad to leave, on the basis that if something now went wrong, she wasn't there so it couldn't be her fault.

It was the first time it hit me that this race was bigger than just me. I was happy in my race bubble. Having Sa there reminded me just how invested she was in this race too. It was impossible for her not to be. She's been there with me every step of the way on this journey, years of sacrifice, putting her dreams aside in order to help me achieve mine. I only wanted to focus on the process, stage by stage, climb by climb. But with Sa there, it was a constant battle to not let my mind wander, and start thinking I could actually win this. It was the realisation that I wanted to do it for her as much as for me.

Something had gone wrong, as it happened, but it was nothing Sa could take responsibility for. At the start of the previous day's stage, Gianni Moscon had got into an argument with the young Fortuneo-Samsic rider Élie Gesbert. At the time we knew nothing about it. Nothing was said to the team as the racing progressed. It wasn't until Luke came into my room that evening that I was aware of its significance.

'G. Do you know Gianni's been kicked out of the race?'

A few minutes later Nico Portal called us together to confirm it. 'Guys, he's out. He's swung an arm at another rider.'

An hour on, and Gianni came to see me. 'I just wanted to say sorry for everything, I shouldn't have done it.'

I asked him what happened. He said he was trying to follow Alejandro Valverde, to keep Valverde in the group and Gesbert had come alongside him and not let him out, and he'd got angry.

I wasn't sure what to tell him. I couldn't say, 'It's alright, mate', because it wasn't alright. You can't do something like that, and if you have Gianni's chequered history, you should be aware of everything you do. 'Mate, that was shit. You need to learn from it and try and deal with your anger. Seriously. See someone about it.'

Gianni's a very promising rider but he's like a bull. He charges at stuff. He has no middle ground. He's either so quiet and shy he can't make eye contact, or something happens and he's seeing red; he'll just flip and say or do something he regrets at the drop of a hat. He's young, and I hope he sorts himself out.

So. We would be down to seven riders. With me and Froomey one and two on GC and a huge week to come, with three days in the mountains likely to see everything thrown at us by our rivals, it was definitely not ideal. Other teams were worse off – AG2R were down to five riders, Katusha to four – but we hadn't lost anyone to injury or crashes or time cuts. It could have been avoided, and that made it worse.

The tight team around Chris and me could quickly start to unravel. Luke wasn't in the best of shape. He hadn't been sleeping too well, not least because he'd had an upset tummy and the subsequent messy backside. We were all nervous for how it might affect him; we were trying to manage his workload on the stage, and he was even travelling in a car, rather than on the team bus, to reduce the risk of anyone else catching his virus. We're not supposed to shake hands with strangers on Tour; we're supposed to offer a fist-bump instead, and then immediately reach for the hand sanitiser when it's polite to do so. The soigneurs even go into our hotel rooms before we do and wipe down the television remote controls with alcohol wipes. At the same time, we couldn't make Luke feel like an outcast, forced to carry a bell around with him to warn of his arrival. Taking the piss seemed to be the best way to deal with the issues of a man who wished he could stop taking so many shits. 'Mate, you've got a big day tomorrow now. 200km in total, so if you cover the first 150km, that would be ideal, yeah?'

Rest days also bring media duties. Because of where Chris and I were on the GC, and because the Tour has a long and dramatic history of riders on the same team falling out in pursuit of the yellow jersey – Hinault v LeMond in 1985, Contador and Armstrong at Astana in 2009, a little something that went on at Sky in 2012 – there was intense interest in how we were getting along, in who was now the team leader, over whether one of us would now attack the other.

We did a joint press conference under a gazebo by the world's smallest hotel swimming pool to the backdrop of cars and lorries battering past on the dual carriageway, while the Carcassonne version of Del Boy tried to sell knock-off versions of Sky jerseys from the back of a van on the street outside. This is the sort of thing that only happens on the Tour. There is often the suspicion that we get a party line to repeat to the media on these occasions, but while George will always ask if we'd like any help, I'd rather just say it as it is. I knew I'd be asked about Gianni, and I knew how I felt: it was stupid, we're all disappointed, there's nothing we can do about it now. I'm worse when I'm told what to say. I can't remember the correct phrases or put them in the right order. If there's something I don't want to talk about, I'll be honest about that as well, and say, I'm sorry, I don't want to talk about that.

Chris and I still hadn't had a conversation about how we'd play it out on the road, except to say we'd let it play out on the road. He still wanted to try to win, and I was pretty sure he was still confident in himself that he could. For me that was fine; if he wanted to attack then he could go and I could follow Dumoulin, just as I had on that initial move on Alpe d'Huez. I reasoned that the other GC guys weren't strong enough to definitely bring him back, but they also were never going to leave him. I could follow them, and then if I could jump across towards the very end of the climb then I'd do that. I had confidence in my legs and I was happier to have a teammate alongside me on the podium rather than rivals stacked up all around. We were the dominant team and we had all the cards to play that we wanted. It was the others who would have to gamble, not us.

Stage 16 that sticky Tuesday was a long one into the Pyrenees but it was almost a warm-up for the mountain challenges that would follow. 218km from Carcassonne to Bagnères-de-Luchon, a second category climb of the Col de Portet d'Aspet, 5.4km at just over 7%, then 6.9km of the Col de Menté at 8%, a brisk descent and up to the top of the Col du Portillon at 1,292m, same sort of gradient, and a nasty technical drop down to the famous old spa town to finish.

On the surface there was nothing spectacular to worry about, yet there were plenty of possible tripwires. The climbs in the Pyrenees are generally different in character to the Alpine ones: steeper, shorter, rougher, heavier, more twisty. The atmosphere on the roadside is different, the passion of the Basque supporters taking away the edge of aggression we'd sometimes found across the first fortnight of racing and bringing the pure love of racing. Put it this way: if I were to go on a hilly summer holiday I would go to the Pyrenees over the Alps.

Bagnères-de-Luchon would be a familiar finishing post, not only because the Tour habitually comes through when in the south-west corner of France, but because we had stayed there on our reconnaissance mission after the Dauphiné. It's famous for its thermal springs, although my memory of it was more specific to the peculiar demands of pro cycling: the hotel where we had stayed had served microwaved scrambled eggs in the morning. I don't want to give the impression that we're divas – although I'm aware that last sentence may have done so – but when you're used to a chef providing excellent, if simple, food, and when your performance in your day-job depends on you eating the right sort of breakfast, then a restaurant where they can't be arsed cooking a dish that takes two ingredients and three minutes definitely harshes your morning vibe.

Breakfast disappointments aside, those recons certainly added to my good mood as we left Carcassonne just before midday. It's not so much that you have a photographic recall at all times of the ascents you are about to take on, or the exact sequence of corners on a descent, but when you are in the fierce moments of a race, the memory is jogged and the red warning lights can flash. On the recon you make a mental note: okay, there's a 180-degree corner after a long straight halfway down. As you come into that section a month later, it all comes back to you. And we had done it properly: riding up from Bagnères to the summit and back down again one day, going up the other side of the climb the following day and down the descent again.

What did disturb the calm was being pepper-sprayed by a policeman as the peloton made its way towards the first climb. On the long list of Things That Could Go Wrong – which included, but was not limited to, crashing, being broken by rivals on a climb, puncturing, getting the shits from Luke, getting a mechanical and being punched by an angry Sky-hating fan – being pepper-sprayed by a riot policeman had not yet figured, not even in Rod Ellingworth's most detailed planning document.

There was little warning. I suppose that is the whole point

with pepper spray, but still. Nico Portal came on the team radio to tell us that there were farmers protesting about a kilometre up the road; there had been bales of hay thrown but our route through was clear, though narrow. We weren't too concerned. Farmers' protests are another Tour staple to go with the television shots of fields of sunflowers or the white horse being ridden bareback alongside us. There used to be an unofficial deal made with the race organisers in the old days, when they were sympathetic to the rural working-class who made up so much of their audience: do your protest, but let's agree to have it here, nice and early in the stage, rather than there, where it'll mess things up for everyone.

What we didn't realise was that the protesters were threatening to go into the road. When the already-twitchy riot police saw this, one officer decided to restrain a woman with pepper spray. Without checking first which way the wind was blowing. Or that the spray would pause in front of the woman, reverse and blow directly into the route of the world's most famous bike riders.

That's strange, I thought, as we zipped past the bales. Something's gone up my nose. Then my eyes started watering, and I noticed a weird taste at the back of my throat that was even more unpleasant than microwaved scrambled eggs.

Accurate information in these scenarios is hard to get hold of. A message went out on the management WhatsApp group from Gary the mechanic: 'The team's just been pepper-sprayed.' Understandably this created a certain amount of disquiet until Nico was able to issue the follow-up: 'It's the whole peloton . . .'

I don't think it was that bad. It was a diluted waft rather than the direct face-full experienced by the protester. I'd go as far as to say that a few guys milked it a bit more than it needed to be. There is one photo of Froomey with his glasses off pouring water into his upturned eyes where his expression makes it appear that he is screaming in pain, which is unfortunate. But the whole race stopped, and there was excited talk of stopping the stage. It was similar to when the fire alarm goes off at school, and as you're all milling about in the playground, one kid starts the rumour that school's being cancelled for the day and you can't let yourself believe it because it'll make the reality of trooping back into the classroom in ten minutes' time all the harder to bear. Nico was straight on the radio: guys, it's not going to happen, so just keep your heads on. Luke was next on. 'I'm at the front here with Gilbert and a few others, they're keen to keep racing so don't start thinking that we won't.'

We parked up for a few moments and tried to regain our dignity. Water was handed out from the team cars to rinse out throats and eyes. I could appreciate why, when you are pepper-sprayed properly, it stops you doing whatever you're doing. But we had only been lightly dusted. It would be a great story for the news bulletins but it would be nothing more than a brief press on the pause button for those of us racing for the hills.

It was a day when the break took a long time to go, which worked for Luke, who had no Gianni to support him and so worked for the team. We were expecting a big day, but the real attacks never came. Gilbert went away on the Col de Portet d'Aspet but that was fine; it was all about a rogue stage win or setting up Julian Alaphilippe rather than the GC. When he crashed, overcooking a corner, slamming into a low wall and disappearing down into the invisible beyond, we were just glad it was only a fractured kneecap rather than anything worse; this was the mountain where Fabio Casartelli had suffered a fatal accident twenty-three years before.

For us, it was almost spookily quiet. Coming into the first climb I had spotted a massive cloud up ahead, black and stormy, but the rain never hit us. We turned right up another valley and it stayed blue overhead and dry under our wheels. Ilnur Zakarin and Jakob Fuglsang had a go at the bottom on the final climb, but we were riding strong, and we knew they couldn't keep riding at that pace all the way. We slowly brought them back, content that the break with Alaphilippe and Adam Yates in it had ten minutes on us because no one in it was interested in stealing my yellow jersey.

Mikel Landa tried a cheeky move going over the top and on the final descent, the first thing Movistar had attempted to spring all day. Kwiato had been ramping up our speed anyway, but Froomey, keen to gain a little more time on Dumoulin, accelerated quickly and passed me and Kwiato. Kwiato kept accelerating and had soon closed the gap to the two of them. Landa had ridden the first few corners hard; when he saw we were all still on his wheel, he slowed up again. Chris was a little annoyed. Why didn't you let me go; I know that descent, we've done it twice already. Less an argument than a passing squall. Just one of those things that happens on a big stage, nobody at fault and nobody hanging on to disagreement too long.

Yates' crash, coming as he was leading Alaphilippe at the front of the race by fifteen seconds, came through to us over the radio. The immediate reaction was one of disappointment for him. He's British, and from what I've seen, a good guy. The second thought was, is this descent a bit sketchy then? Is it wetter down there than we knew, more dangerous than our recon may have been?

Nico helped us out. Back in the team car, it can be hard for him to know exactly where we are on a descent. But he could jog our collective memories: guys, don't forget the tight bend at eight kilometres to go; Yates has gone down on a left-hander, stay alert.

The tripwires never materialised. Alaphilippe took his second stage win of the race, profiting from Adam's misfortune. Chris and I and those behind us rolled in together, my lead constant over Froomey at one minute and thirty-nine seconds, Dumoulin at one fifty. Primož Roglič at two thirty-eight, Romain Bardet at three twenty-one.

In Gianni's absence, I felt the strength of the team that day. There were no egos. If someone was feeling bad, they said so and someone else stepped up. Someone was always having a good day: Kwiato on La Rosière, Egan on Alpe d'Huez. That was absolutely critical for me as well; I wasn't having to do any more work than I had to. A good day to get ticked off, a good vibe to take into the thriller to follow.

Chapter Thirteen

Everyone Must Be Hurting

Wednesday, 25 July. Stage 17, the start of the Tour on the Vendée two and a half weeks before now feeling an awful long way off. If ever there was a day to prove that length matters less than what you do with it, this would be it: just sixty-five kilometres to ride, but two category 1 climbs followed by an absolute giant.

It would be the shortest road stage at a Tour since I had been born. Sixty-five kilometres? That's nothing. That's an after-work spin for a club rider. Unless forty-three kilometres of that is uphill, and sixteen of those forty-three kilometres are at an average gradient of more than 8%, and the final climb is up a road so steep and distant that it has never been raced up before . . .

There would be a different start to normal, a gimmick. We riders would be gridded accorded to our position on the GC, as if we were F1 cars – me alone on the front row, Froomey and Tom Dumoulin on the next row, Primož Roglič, Romain Bardet and Mikel Landa on the next and onwards until the end. The theory was that we would be isolated from our loyal domestiques, be forced to ride alone and come under immediate attack. The reality we weren't entirely certain of but we felt it might not be quite as thrilling.

It wasn't like you needed to force the drama. Straight out of the blocks, gridded or otherwise, we would be unleashed up the Col de Peyresourde and its second helping, the Montée de Peyragudes. Topping a 1,645m summit just 15km into a stage was radical and it was nasty, particularly when the climb averaged close to 7%. A descent, and then straight up the Col de Val Louron-Azet, 7.4km at 8.3%. That was the warm-up. Into our sights would then come the Col du Portet, except it was so long and steep that only a small portion of it would actually be visible. The highest mountain in the entire race, all the way up to 2,215m on a road that averaged 8.7% along its 16km length, had frequent ramps of more than 10% and for most of its life had been unpaved and covered, in places, with cow pat.

'It's as difficult as Mont Ventoux,' the organisers had announced proudly, which is the sort of thing that puts a smile on the faces of Tour watchers and a shiver through those riding it. We had recce'd it on that same trip that had taken us along yesterday's stage 16 and Saturday's upcoming time-trial course over towards Biarritz, and I was glad we had. This, for sure, was the hardest single climb of the race. The first part was proper steep. There was a relative breather around 8km, if you consider a 500m section at 5% to be a breather, and then it reverted to being horrific and relentless once again. All at altitude, too, a test of our Teide training like nothing we had come across before. It was a short day and it was a big, big day too.

How would we tackle it? Physically we would treat it like a time-trial day. An hour and a bit ride to the start in the morning, which was up and down the final climb of the previous day. Then a good warm-up on the turbos before the start. A couple of coffees and away we go. Focus on the process and what we have to do.

What were we going to do? That was the stuff that hadn't come up on the recon. The night before, there was a little talk around the team that Froomey might attack at the bottom of the final climb. I asked Dave Brailsford and Tim Kerrison about it individually and was reassured that they felt the same way I did, that the tactic was too risky for both of us. An attack early on the Portet, twelve kilometres out from the finish, might make sense if Chris was the only one in contention for the yellow jersey. The danger as I saw it was that Dumoulin then dropped me and either caught Chris, thanks to the target dangled in front of him, or got close and left me a minute and fifteen seconds down. Suddenly both of us would be within twenty seconds of Dumoulin, and the time trial on Saturday would be a lot tighter than it had to be.

I could understand what Froomey was trying to achieve. He was a four-time champion with a winner's head on his shoulders. The ambition was there to win another and draw level with those four greats, Anquetil, Merckx, Hinault and Induráin. He has always had that self-belief, and when he gets something in his head he sticks at it. This time he had it in his head that if he went early then that was the way he could distance Dumoulin, that Dumoulin wouldn't be able to ride that pace from the bottom. He wasn't thinking that he might over-cook himself in the process, that no one could ride that hard that early, that he might then crack further up.

I wasn't quite sure why no one from the management team was discussing it any further. During the team meeting on the bus that Wednesday morning, Nico gave a relatively straightforward speech: don't mess it up, guys, don't attack each other; make sure we win, because if we don't win, Luke is going to be annoyed.

I nodded. Yes, okay. So what's the plan on the final climb?

There wasn't one. That was it. I took Luke aside afterwards. Was it just me, or was that meeting weird? So we're riding like we always do but then on the last climb, there's no plan? Froomey's free to attack?

We rode to the start, Chris and I alongside each other. I told Chris my concerns. G, it'll be fine. Don't worry about it, I'm doing this.

It bothered me. The risk of it, not the fact Froomey wanted to see what he could do. Were management reluctant to tell him, or did they really feel he could pull it off? He isn't often told what to do. Maybe they didn't want to upset him. He'd won six Grand Tours. He deserved a chance. At the same time, there comes a point where you need to say, no, this is what's happening, and no, you're not allowed to do this or that.

It made more sense to me to wait until 5km to go. It wasn't like it got any easier at that point; you'd be at a nasty altitude, and everyone would be tired. In those circumstances, you can really make a difference; I had put 22 seconds into Dumoulin at La Rosière in 800m. At the end of a 16km climb at altitude, if you had the legs and you went with 2.5km to go, you could get close to a minute if you were strong and your rival wasn't.

There was another thing that was puzzling me. It seemed like a lot of risk just to take second place. Maybe management were confident that I would be okay whatever happened and that I would stay in first. I wasn't sure what other team would be as concerned about gambling for a one-two if it meant that one would be less certain. It was good to give Chris his chance, but at the same time, why didn't I deserve my chance to be fully protected?

I'm not a stresser. I wasn't angry. It was just the logical part of my brain working away. There was nothing to be gained from worrying about it. My form was great, my confidence was high. If Froomey goes, it's a bit risky and Dumoulin might gap me. But why should Dumoulin drop me? Okay. Go if you want. We'll deal with it. I'm going to follow Dumoulin and stay strong and just keep doing what I've been doing.

I didn't feel as if it were threatening our relationship. At the Tour you logically become more about the professional bond rather than the personal one. We were all immersed in our own little worlds and how we dealt with it all. Three weeks later, training together, it had flipped around. The personal was now the dominant part. Chris would ask if Sa and I fancied an afternoon on the beach with him and his son Kellan. In the guts of the biggest bike race of all, it has to be different. You don't win six Grand Tours by not having confidence in yourself and being aggressive.

It's one of the peculiar charms of cycling. There are very few sports where you're a teammate with someone but also their rival, where what's best for you may be to do what's worst for them. Maybe in middle- and long-distance running, or in a triathlon. I wasn't upset that Froomey wanted to do it. The only thing that troubled me was the reason he was doing it. Was he attacking to beat Dumoulin, or was he attacking to win the race? If it was the second of the two, he was by default attacking me.

It played on my mind. I realised that was why I was a little miffed with the team as well. Guys, is he attacking here to win? Because if he's attacking to win, I may chase him. I'm not just going to let him win. If we go into the start and say, look, we're racing against each other, then fair enough, all in. But if I'm letting you get a gap here, and you're going to use that gap to try and take the yellow jersey off me ... If that's what happening, I'm not going to let you do that.

Based on the way the race had been up to that Wednesday and the way I thought we all were, I was confident that Dumoulin was strong and it wouldn't just be a case of watching Froomey ride off the road. Everyone was going to chase him, and I was confident that if I needed to, I'd be able to jump up across to him. Even if I could, I decided that I wouldn't do it early on. I'd wait until right up close to the line, confident that I could get thirty seconds back in the last kilometre or two, and that way not taking anyone else with me either. That might help Chris move up the GC or extend his cushion too over those chasing him.

I blocked the rest of it out. Don't worry about the permutations as they happen. Keep everything as simple as possible. Maybe it would actually work out better for me, if I were to hold on all the way to Paris, that Chris had been given his head. If team orders had been that he couldn't attack me, then there might always have been a narrative that he let me win. Maybe it would be better for me that he did exactly what he wanted, his way, and wasn't strong enough to do it.

Critically, neither of us was taking it personally. This was nothing like those famous intra-team rivalries of the past. Chris knew I wanted to win and I knew Chris wanted to win so it was never underhand. Both of us were being honest. He had won four Tours in five years. It would have been stranger if he'd said I'm an ambitious bloke, I've won six Grand Tours, yet I'm not going to try to win this one. Of course he wanted to win. It was entirely natural.

To the start, and the only damp squib on a day of fireworks. The grid system looked great and did nothing. We all rolled away at exactly the same pace as always. Luke had been nervous because he was right at the back, thanks to his position in the GC, and had to try to get to the front as soon as possible, but it turned out to be a really controlled start. That was the way it was always going to go, but I was sat there thinking, this is perfect. Over the top of the Montée de Peyragudes, the first of the three big climbs, with the status quo right where it was, the descent stress-free. For now.

It began for real on the Col de Val Louron-Azet. AG2R hit it hard, Pierre Latour going to the front for Bardet. It was too much too soon; there was no way they could keep riding at 450 watts all the way to the summit, and I had to remind myself of that. This is hard, this is hard, but stick here for now, stay strong. They're never going to keep up like this, soon enough they'll slow down …

They tried spiking the pace out of the hairpins. Froomey has done it before, burning his rivals repeatedly, and I guessed they were trying to do the same. We let the gap go and worked on it Dumoulin-style, hard pace but constant, avoiding flicking the needle into the red. Trying to relish the challenge rather than fearing it. They were riding fast, whoa, he must be feeling good, we've got a race on our hands. Thinking too: this is what my lead has done to them. They feel they have to do something different, even if it's illogical, even if it's the wrong thing. Bardet had already lost half his team, and he was hurting the rest of them now too. Latour was pulling a heroic shift at the front, throwing his bike everywhere, yet he would be toast long before the final climb.

Through the ski resort of Saint-Lary-Soulan, Julian Alaphilippe and the Estonian Tanel Kangert leading on to the Col du Portet with two and a half minutes to us in the peloton. An attack from Dan Martin and Nairo Quintana from behind us – let 'em go, guys, keep it steady, this is not the killer move. Jonathan Castroviejo leading our line, all of us settling in. Quintana dropping Dan and starting to hoover up the splintered remains of the break up the road.

You know the attacks are coming, and you have to respond with your brain as much as your legs. Less than three kilometres into the climb, Roglič had his first dig. Froomey jumped onto his wheel. Dumoulin went to the front of our group and began the chase.

It was early to go and it was hurting both Chris and Roglič. I could see Chris pulling a turn or two at the front too, and that set off alarm bells. Onto the team radio. 'Froomey. Don't ride, especially now Roglič has attacked. Just sit on him. Use him. If you do feel good, go over the top, don't just ride with him.'

I could see they were in danger of burning each other out. Dumoulin loves these relentless pursuits. It's like he hauls himself up the mountain on a cable. The pace almost never jumps, but he never slows either. It doesn't look as flashy as Bardet's dancing in the pedals or Alaphilippe's musketeer moves but he is always there at the end when the dazzling boys may not be. It hurts others, too. Our group was shedding exhausted riders with each one hundred metres. Soon it was Tom, me, Egan Bernal, Mikel Landa, Bardet and Steven Kruijswijk. Within another minute, Tom had brought us back to Roglič and Chris too. He knows what he's doing. It works.

The Portet teases you and it taunts you. You climb fast and you can see Saint-Lary down in the valley below you, and you look ahead and see what must be the top. All is sunshine and green trees and prettiness. And then you swing right and the valley disappears and you see a whole new heap of mountain up ahead, the road twisting and turning like a tourniquet, and you remember that it goes on, and on – up as far as the end of a ski lift, curling round the start of another, smaller cable car, away over slopes that are now bare except for scrubby pasture and bare rock. It's a mountain to wreck ambitions and to shove the truth into your face: if you've got it, you will fly; if you have cracks, they will blow apart.

Quintana was travelling. Through Valverde and his small group, up to Kangert, Rafał Majka caught. Soon it was Quintana on his own with Dan Martin close and we GC men a minute off, fighting our own private war.

Wout Poels had come to the party. Bardet, shattered from his earlier efforts, was the first of the big boys to blow out the back. Through eight kilometres to go, seven, six. A jump from Kruijswijk, the other half of the jab-hook Lotto NL-Jumbo combo after Roglič had swung first. That briefly distanced Wout, and Egan took over the reins momentarily until Wout fought his way back; he was pulling some shift.

Five kilometres. Froome at the back of the group with Dumoulin, Tom there because he was marking Chris, Chris there because his legs were starting to betray him.

Then they started to play a few mind games. Dumoulin dropping off the back of the group momentarily. Froomey straight on the radio: 'Dumoulin is struggling. Wout – pick it up!' I was straight on the radio. 'No, boys, chill. Just keep this pace as it is. Still five kilometres to go. If he's getting dropped at this pace, why speed up?' He was starting to drift off the last wheel, trying to ride it conservatively but realising too that he had to stay or be gone for good. A sprint to the front from Froomey, Dumoulin following him, thinking he was attacking. Dumoulin was fine. A minute on, and Chris lowered his chin towards the little mic we all have halfway down our team radio cables. 'I'm not feeling super. Slow down a bit.'

It's cruel, but when I heard that I just got so much confidence from it. If Froomey was struggling now, then everyone must be hurting. I felt like I was getting better as we got higher.

Man, I'm going to smash them today . . .

Three kilometres to the summit, and Roglič went again. The Lotto lads were really going for this, taking it in turns to dish out the punishment. A sign that he had recognised the hell that Froomey was going through, a knife in an open wound. Egan worked us back up to his wheel. I could follow quite comfortably, but when we glanced back, we realised Chris and Landa had not made the move with us. In that moment I knew. This was mine now. Whatever had been said that morning, whatever subconscious deference there may been within me or the team and the management, I was the dominant one now. I was the leader.

Dumoulin with a final dart. I followed him with confidence and ease. Just Roglič and Kruijswijk with me, Roglič going again, me closing that one again as Tom laboured for the first time and Kruijswijk began to fade too.

1,000m to go. Quintana up the road by half a minute from Dan and fifty seconds from us. Chill now, I'll just wait until the last 200m and kick one more time.

It was that easy. What an amazing feeling to have, what a sense of uncomplicated power. In those last 200m, I put five seconds into Roglič and Dumoulin. Four more seconds for coming in third in the stage behind Quintana and Dan. I thought back to Froomey and his gamble as he laboured in, another forty-eight seconds down on me, wondering what would have happened if he had waited at the bottom, if he had saved what he had, rather than thrown it away when we still had so far to go . . .

Maybe it would have made no difference. He was not on a great day anyway. Maybe I didn't need to worry about it. Every day I was feeling stronger, feeling more invincible. This is like dreamland. This is everything coming together, when everyone is saying I will fall apart.

The night before I had thought that holding my current lead over Dumoulin would be a dream. Instead I had extended it further still. It was now a minute and fifty-nine seconds, Froome two and a half minutes down in third, Roglič fourth at two forty-seven. Quintana, in fifth, was three and a half minutes back.

And it could have been more. In the final hundred metres, as I went away on my own, a man reached out across the barriers on the right-hand side of the road. In the moment I thought it was just some over-exuberant fan waving whose hand had inadvertently caught me. I was out the saddle and wobbled a little and I looked back, thinking, what the hell was that? Only when I saw it afterwards in a photograph did I realise that he had actually tried to grab my arm, that had he not underestimated how fast I was travelling and how slick my arm was with sweat, then he could have brought me down.

Pepper spray from a cop, a tackle from a pissed-up idiot. It was in danger of becoming ridiculous. We would have to ride in the middle of the road, and why should we need to race in a certain part of the road in case some idiot makes us crash? One of the elements I'd always loved about cycling was how open and free it is. As a fan you can rock up to the start and see your heroes ride past you less than a metre away. You can watch us warming up, close enough to be able to hear the breath rasping and smell the sweat on the jerseys. But imagine the outrage if Rafa Nadal's arm was grabbed as he was winding up his forehand, or Gareth Bale shoved as he ran up to take a free kick. It couldn't happen, and it shouldn't happen in cycling either.

Froomey's own day would get worse when a gendarme failed to recognise him as he made the descent from the finish line and pulled him off his bike, sending him sprawling. That might have sent many riders to bed in an exhausted grump, but not Chris. An hour or so later, in the kitchen truck as we piled food onto our plates, he took me aside and gave me a big hug.

'Congratulations, mate. I didn't get the chance at the finish to say well done properly, but good job. I'm really happy for you. Genuinely.'

It was a special moment. At the same time, part of me felt sorry for him. Not because I was winning, but because he was so obviously disappointed with how he was doing. I wanted him to finish second behind me, yet he had dropped down another place on the GC. For him to be able to say that he was glad I was still in yellow would have taken a lot in the normal world, and even more for a serial winner like him, one Tour win from levelling up history.

It also made me reassess some of the questions I had asked myself earlier in the day. Chris definitely wanted to win that day and to win the Tour. But he wasn't attacking to stop me winning. He was doing what great champions do.

He went further before the night was done. Geraint, he told the world's media, is now our number one. For the next three days, I'm riding for him.

He hadn't needed to say that either. But it helped me on the road, and it would help me off it. No more questions about our rivalry, about who would bow to whom. We all had our answer.

Chapter Fourteen

Through the Clouds

Every hard day that was ticked off, a little more confidence. I wasn't surprised to be in yellow, because I always thought there was a chance. It was more surprising how I was winning. I felt in control the whole time. I never rode out and thought, this is the day it could slip away. I had won Paris–Nice in 2016 by four seconds from Alberto Contador, and there had been the most almighty chase in the final hour of racing to keep my precious lead. I imagined that to win the Tour you'd have to go through a similarly angst-ridden experience – just about get over the line. But first at the Dauphiné and now here at the Tour, I was feeling in control. Not comfortable, because it's always hard, but never thinking that Dumoulin or Froomey or Quintana or whoever was going to drop me. To have that mindset in this race was crazy. I felt great in the Alps. I felt great after Mende. The Pyrenees were treating me well so far and my belief was growing with every attack I followed.

Thursday, 26 July should have been easy. 171km from Trie-sur-Baïse to Pau, only two fourth category climbs to deal with, the brief Côte de Madiran – just over a kilometre at 7% – and the Côte d'Anos, its 2.1km at 4.6% hardly any more of a challenge. Stage 18 was one for the sprinters after the hills and thrills of the last two up-and-down days.

Should have been easy. At the finish, Tim Kerrison would tell us it was one of the three easiest days we had ridden all Tour. That's not good for morale, I would reply. It would be one of my most uncomfortable days of all, a heat in the air that suffocated like a steaming blanket, the pace just always a fraction too high. I was hoping I was going to feel like the stage to Valence the day after Alpe d'Huez, when it was easy but fast. This was what we call grippy. I enjoyed only two aspects: the start, and the finish.

These days get messy. So many of the big-name sprinters had gone that no one was quite sure which denuded team would take it up at the front. A break went away fine. UAE, thinking about Alexander Kristoff, and FDJ, all about Arnaud Démare, came to the front to control. The only issue was they kept the break way too close to the peloton, fluctuating between forty-five seconds and a minute thirty. Do that and others in the peloton will start to get ideas. Sure enough, Sep Vanmarcke and Jasper Stuyven put in a massive attack up a drag and tried to jump across, and that kicked it all off in the peloton. For no real reason, which makes it hurt so much more.

Anger ricocheted around. 'Boys, you could have just let it go out to two, two and a half minutes, and it would have been fine!' We all wanted to ride easy. But there was too much panic in others' minds, too little strategy. FDJ could have blown it for Démare. With twenty kilometres to go, a good group of around ten guys were off the front of the peloton. That amount of fresh guys so close to the finish could easily make it all the way. The group contained some strong men, Dan Martin, Jack Bauer and Simon Clarke. Luke Rowe had to work hard with a few others to bring it all back together.

It's baffling sometimes when teams haven't really had to control before and suddenly have to try it – the tactics, the communication. It's not just about your super-domestiques, having seven, eight strong guys . . . that is the biggest difference between us and a lot of the other teams. We've got some of the best riders in the world when you look at them individually, but it's the way you ride together that matters. If it's not shown properly on television, you don't realise. You think there's a little gap and then three kilometres later it's closed. You don't see what happens.

It was more mentally tiring than physically, that sort of niggly pace where you're not quite in control any more, where if it were ten or twenty watts less it would suddenly feel a lot easier. Had it been us setting that tempo, it might have felt okay, but when someone else is doing it to you, it always feels that little bit harder. It was also a day bracketed by two mountainous monsters, a stage when I wasn't really going to do anything – harder to get yourself up for, still switched on and aware of everything, but nowhere near like the day before. There were a few corners towards the end where I even let a few guys come round me, which meant as Démare won the sprint up ahead, I would finish back in thirty-first, the lowest placing I would have all Tour. I'd never have done that earlier in the contest. But once I was into the final three kilometres, my time safe no matter what crash might come, I thought, okay, it's alright now. Just try to save every little bit of energy I've got.

Friday, 27 July. In two days we would be in Paris, but we were a long way that morning from the wide boulevards and small yappy dogs and the things that small yappy dogs leave on boulevard pavements. Stage 19, taking the long and scenic route from Lourdes to Laruns, 4,800m of climbing across 200km of racing and 7 categorised climbs. It was a gruesome mug-shot line-up of all the big hitters – the Col d'Aspin, 12km at 6.5%, the monstrous Col du Tourmalet, 17.1km at 7.3% and the Col d'Aubisque, 16.6km at 4.9%. We would finish by plummeting 1,200m over 20km down into the finish line, exactly the sort of descent that I knew would have my family and supporters almost unable to watch for fear of what might transpire.

The day's route looked like a horrible broken figure-of-eight. Of the 176 riders who had begun racing almost three weeks before, we were down to 146. It was time to think about survival rather than flourishing; every man was exhausted, the ones out in front just slightly less exhausted than all the others.

Get through the stage, don't lose any time, stick together. We knew it was probably going to kick off on the Tourmalet, but we didn't expect it to explode quite as early as it did. There was also the time trial to worry about on Saturday, so while the top five riders on the GC might want to go all in, they might want to hold something back, too. One problem:

no longer was this just about the yellow jersey. There was a fist fight going on for all the places down below the top three, so when Bob Jungels got in the break for Quick-Step to try to get into the top ten on GC, Katusha decided to jump to the front of the bunch to bring it back for their man Ilnur Zakarin. We had been quite happy with the break. No threats, no worries. And then what we thought would be a big day became a whole lot tougher.

It was typical desperate stuff for the last few days of the Tour, when everyone wants to protect their position. Katusha were riding full gas on the flat, and they only had four riders left in the entire race. We weren't sure if they were trying to bring the break back or bring it close so it might kick off on the first climb so Zakarin could go away, but it was ballsy and it hurt. There are tricks you can play in that scenario, and Luke tried one of them: starting to ride with them on the climb, and then knocking ten watts off the power to surreptitiously slow it down. Unfortunately, they spotted pretty quickly what he was trying to do. So they ended up riding hard all the way to the bottom of the Tourmalet. Magic.

You had to hand it to Katusha. As soon as we hit the climb, Ian Boswell popped in a cheeky attack with Zakarin. Mikel Landa and Romain Bardet got themselves involved in the attacks too. Stay calm, boys. There was a hell of a long way to go. To go all the way up the Tourmalet, a long descent into the valley and then up the Aubisque as well with a lead still intact, would take something phenomenal, as well as a series of dramatic errors from us. We were happy to let them go out to two minutes or so over the summit, leaving Castro and Wout to set a decent tempo to stop the lead shooting out.

When you are wearing yellow, there is always someone more desperate than you. So when the group out front had a lead of three minutes going onto the Col des Bordères, the second category climb forty-odd kilometres from the finish, Landa was still a minute shy of going into the virtual race lead, but awfully close to stealing the top five standing of Primož Roglič and Steven Kruijswijk.

There were good riders up there, Bardet too. Those boys could work together. But I knew that even should Landa take the yellow jersey off me today, he'd still need another minute or so advantage over me going into the time trial – probably more, because if he did take the lead, today would be a big, big day for him with a price to pay for it the next. And by letting the gap go as we did, it forced LottoNL-Jumbo to ride instead.

You expect a team going to the front to set a high tempo. Robert Gesink did exactly that for Roglič and Kruijswijk. You expect it too to settle down. But Gesink, who had done little all race except get in the occasional breakaway, set a really strong pace from the bottom of the descent until the start of the last climb up the Aubisque. That strong tempo in turn put Wout and Castro on their limits, and when Roglič attacked soon after, Kwiato only had a little left to give, too.

I was hurting. I was tired. At the same time, I knew that I could follow Dumoulin, and I never felt like I was going to lose his wheel. That was all I had to do. He was strong enough to respond to all of Roglič's attacks. Perfect.

Froomey was struggling once again. Towards the top, he was distanced from our group, and as we crested the Col du Soulor, which makes up most of the Aubisque, I wondered whether the other three – Dumoulin, Roglič and Kruijswijk – might gang up on me, and in doing so, really put Chris in the deep stuff. There was a little flatter section before the final kick up to the top of the Aubisque. Froomey had Egan drop back to him, and the chance was there.

They never took it. Maybe Kruijswijk was annoyed that Roglič had attacked behind when he had a little gap. Sod it, you pull more now since you jumped across to me. At one point I did hear Dumoulin tell Roglič that he wouldn't attack him, as if he wanted them to ride together and keep Froome out of the top three. These quick deals and counter-offers go on all the time when you're deep in a Grand Tour and trying to grab anything to keep afloat. Sometimes they stick. This one didn't. Without the injection of pace, Egan was able to tow Chris back up, and we were all together once again.

For me, watching the bloke closest in the GC make deals to beat the bloke in fourth rather than attack the one man above him was a lovely feeling. I was so in control of the race those last seven days, and had been able to respond to everything they had tried, that maybe they had reached the end point: there's nothing we can really do to hurt him now, so let's defend what we have.

It was exhilarating. Come on, show me. Do whatever you can. I can respond every time now.

We caught Zakarin before the summit, the sun now gone, thick clouds settling on the steep slopes around us. Landa, Bardet and Majka ahead, but only just, and when Roglič leapt across to them, Tom had to chase him to protect his own second place, and I could follow him all the way.

Onto the descent. Twenty kilometres to survive, in the mist, only a time trial to come. Just keep concentrating, take it corner by corner.

It was probably the most stressful half-hour of the entire three weeks after the first fifty kilometres of the Roubaix stage. I had a good advantage. There was no reason for me to take any risks. But Roglič and Dumoulin were still racing full gas and risking, and I was stuck between wanting to take it easy, and not wanting to show any weakness and let them drift off and gain thirty seconds.

Just over the crest, Majka had attacked. Roglič got past him. Dumoulin got past him. Majka ahead of me, and a sudden flashback to the Tour twelve months before, and Majka's crash right in front, me smashing into him, and my race being over.

I just shouted. I don't even know what I shouted. Internally, all guns were blazing. Shit. Get round him as quickly as possible. Just stay on that wheel of Dumoulin. Don't let it go anywhere.

You have to relax on a descent. The scarier it is, the more relaxed you have to be. The more you think about things going wrong, the more likely they will. The more you imagine, the more you stiffen up – your body, your torso – and then you don't go around the corners smoothly.

You're jerking, cutting a fifty-pence-piece shape rather than carving a smooth line.

There were two corners where I tightened up. I came into them quicker than I wanted and out of them shakier. That could have been interesting . . .

You try to read the men ahead of you. Roglič was going for the stage win. Tom marking him. I could watch Roglič up ahead, see how he was seeing the road, dab a brake if suddenly he was throwing the bike, shift my weight if he was leaning in more as the corner tightened up. I had my Garmin and its map on the handlebar stem in front of my nose, but I didn't want to look at that too much; we were going so fast that if I took my eyes off the road for even two seconds a bend could be upon me. The straights were not safe. Look down and the next thing you're in the corner before you even look back up.

Looking ahead all the time, as far down the road as possible, even in a corner. Nothing else. Not even thinking, 'This is fast, I don't really want to go this fast, what happens if . . .' Everything is about straight ahead.

Somebody told me afterwards there was a camera angle being shown on television, looking at the back of the group, and Zakarin – never the prettiest of descenders – was on the edge, his lines not quite right, his entry into the corners as squeaky as his brakes. I knew Sa would be unable to watch, that her mum, Beth, would take Blanche, our dog, for a walk somewhere, that my mum and dad would be anywhere but in front of the television, too. No control for them, nothing they can do about it. They wouldn't know that I was feeling good. All those doubts and past disasters would come rushing into their heads.

At least it was dry. As we swished through the bends, dropping the metres away in our slipstream, the clouds were left back up the Aubisque. Down into the dark green valley, the road in front of us pale grey rather than black and treacherous.

Once we got out of the mist, you could see more clearly where you were going. Now I saw that Roglič had a gap, but not how he had worked it. Tom would complain in the aftermath that he had drafted behind one of the television motorbikes, but anyone would do that – you just follow the bike as tight as you can, and if it's too close, then lucky you. Every rider would do it.

I ticked off the last few bends. No calamitous crash today, not for me. A surge of relief, a big, big box ticked.

We had a kilometre and a half of flat along the valley floor before the finish line. Tom was flicking his elbow, trying to get me to come through and take a turn on the front. Roglič was no threat to me; Tom, I could tell, was hurting; he'd swing over and stop pedalling, and then one or two seconds later he would go again. Froomey came up and gave him a few turns. Don't give him too much, mate, make sure he does the majority of it. Just for tomorrow, too, take that little bit extra out of him.

Into the sprint, Roglič for the win and the ten bonus seconds, six more on offer for the man who would take second. I laid off Dumoulin with 400m to go: my plan, if it was possible, was to help Froomey gain a few extra seconds.

But he didn't have the legs, so I went myself, leaving it as late as possible because of a slight headwind, taking a little run at Tom, straight past him and straight through the line.

I was almost frustrated, rather than relieved, caught up momentarily in the racing rather than the big picture. Why did Tom have to lose Roglič's wheel on that descent? I could have gone for another stage win. Just relax, let him do everything, and try to finish it off the next day.

And hey, I was the burglar of the bonus second once again. Their cumulative effect may have been great for my GC lead but their psychological impact was also valuable. It kept my foot on the jugular of my rivals. In boxing terms, I was keeping them on the ropes, never giving them a chance to rally. In stag-do terms, I was the first one to finish my pint in every round. I wasn't actually drinking any more pints than anyone else, but I was controlling the tempo of it all. Every time I put my empty pint glass down on the table with a little clunk, the others were left thinking, oh my God, he's finished his before us again . . .

That night I knew I was a time trial away from winning the Tour de France. I was in the best time-trialling form of my life. So I had a very British conversation about it with Sara on the phone.

'Well done.'

'Yeah, thanks.'

'Just one more day . . .'

'Yeah, we'll see what happens.'

'Which sofa do you prefer then?'

'Er, the first one.'

To bed thinking not of outcomes but of processes. The mentality of the Olympic track rider, going over how I would ride the time trial, not what would happen if I did it well. There are no guarantees in cycling. Secretly, deep inside, I was smiling. I fancied winning another stage.

Rod Ellingworth

I was on absolute tenterhooks when Geraint was coming off the top of the Aubisque. I'd manned an extra feed station for the team on the ascent; they'd gone past me and he looked pretty strong. I didn't have any doubt about what he could do physically, but we were getting reports back from other guys in the team on the descent that it was wet in places under the trees.

I've talked to G a lot over the years about fast descents, about his confidence on them, and I was really feeling for him. I could imagine what was going through his mind: physically I know I can beat them, but something could happen and it would be completely out of my control. We were watching the television coverage in the team car, holding our breath every time he entered a corner – 'Just relax, G, relax the shoulders, relax, relax ...' They put pressure on him. They tried to break him, which is part of the sport – you put pressure on people on descents. The consequences can be drastic, but that's part of the game.

As he hit the bottom, the flat section to the finish, all of us in the car, we let out a massive cheer. We shook hands and we had a little bit of a celebration. 'Other than a time trial, he's done. Physically I think we're there.' That was a great little moment, to be honest.

Chapter Fifteen

Hands Off the Bar

I love a time trial. Ask Rod Ellingworth and he'll say I've got a nice, small frontal area, which in cycling aerodynamics terms is quite the compliment. I enjoyed time trials as a kid and I loved racing the amended team pursuit version at those two Olympics. My final competitive outing before the Tour had been to win the British national title.

I knew this one inside out too. 31km from Saint-Pée-Sur-Nivelle to Espelette, a mad wiggle-waggle through the guts of the French Basque country, 20km south of Biarritz, about 10km inland from the wild and wet Atlantic coast. It was no flat cruise on the tri-bars, but instead a constant series of technical turns and stiff little climbs, including one 900m drag at more than 10% up the Col de Pinodieta. I'd reconned it after the Dauphiné in June when the roads had been open to traffic and I'd been tired and not in the best shape, initially just one lap to see it all, cruise the corners, get a feel for it. A second lap picking up the speed, not to race-pace because of the cars and pedestrians, but cutting a few cute lines through corners, being able to visualise what it would be like when cleared only for us. And then a third for good measure. It's all about the prep.

Early that morning, Saturday, 28 July, we rode it again as a team. It refreshed our memories without taking anything from the legs and lungs, thinking, right, around this sort of power for the first section, use this bit as recovery, then hit this power on this climb. By then you know exactly how you're going to ride it.

The early morning riding was the fun bit. The hanging around, waiting, waiting, was the real challenge. The time trial would go off in reverse order to the general classification, meaning there would be four and a half hours between Lawson Craddock rolling down the start ramp and me riding off to face destiny. My start time wasn't until almost 4.30 p.m. That's a long time to sit about wondering, a long time looking out of the window at the squally Atlantic showers and hoping they blew themselves out over the afternoon.

Our team hotel was more than an hour's drive from the start. Rather than shuttling us around in the bus, the team booked a hotel much closer for Chris and me, the two riders latest off. A tiny little room, just big enough for a shower and a bed, so I could go feet-up as I watched Netflix and listened to a few podcasts, a strange place to spend the day of what might be your cycling coronation. Food three and a half hours before my start time, a last meal: more rice and chicken, getting quite hard to eat by then. I'd eaten so much of the same meal that I almost had to force it down. Burger tonight if I pull this off.

The day had begun with a downpour, moved to showery and then started to dry up, at least until another black maritime cloud dumped another load of rain over the course. In a summer of constant heat, I just wanted a few more hours of blue sky. Even grey would do, just like summer holidays as a kid. Be kind to me for a few more hours and then unleash hell, if you have to.

I spoke to Tim Kerrison. We had broken up the course into seven sections and worked out how I should ride on each chunk, when to try to recover a little and when to push on. The first climb, the rolling bit to the third little descent and to the first checkpoint. When I rode the team pursuit in Olympic finals and world championships, I would visualise the whole race over and over: the start, my first turn on the front and then the second. I was doing the same now, shutting my eyes but seeing the road unfurling in front of me, picturing the curves coming up, leaning my bike into them. Trying to stay in that cool, logical zone and not let my mind drift. Sunday's stage into Paris would be a processional one for the GC contenders. The sprint boys would fight for the stage win, but whoever was in yellow tonight would stay in it. I couldn't let any of that seep in. Start thinking that this was the day I could win the Tour de France and it would be easy to start to crumble. That same boring motto: process not outcome, process, process.

I pulled on my yellow skinsuit early, made sure all the numbering was pinned neatly and straight. A flapping paper race number disturbs the flow of air over your back. A flapping number could cost you the race. Don't think about negatives, just do it right.

Walk to the bus. Make sure you have everything set up around you, in your space, all organised, that you know where everything is. It's all a lot easier when you get on the turbo-trainer to begin your warm-up. That's your normality, a routine you've been through a hundred times. Once again you're just a cyclist, pedalling a bike, feeling your legs warm up and your breathing getting deep and long. You are on automatic, a robot working through its programs.

I didn't feel special or anything. I wasn't overly tired, but nor was I ready to tear the bike off its mounts. Hey, it was stage 20 of the Tour de France. You're always going to feel a bit of heaviness in the legs. It didn't faze me. Finish the warm-up, dry yourself down, go for a last wee. Pull on your mitts, squeeze into your helmet.

I walked off the bus and clipped my aero visor onto the helmet. A chorus of 'good luck' from the lads, pats on the back. Away you go.

I sat at the start, awaiting my turn. Froomey rolling away, Primož Roglič next. Tom Dumoulin was sat there, the last man off before me. He shook my hand. 'Good luck, man. Stay safe.' He seemed genuine about it, too. 'Yeah, have a good one, mate. Let's see what happens . . .' Waiting, waiting. Tom standing up and waddling in his cleats towards his bike and the electronic beeps. Now just me, waiting, trying to visualise it all, desperate to start, desperate to be a cyclist in a simple world of speed and skill rather than a thirty-two-year-old man in unbecomingly tight clothing sitting sweating on a plastic chair.

My turn. Onto the bike, held upright by a commissaire.

Holding the outer parts of the handlebars. Deep breaths. The beeps, spiking the adrenaline. Three. Two. One. Go, go, go . . .

As soon as I rolled down the ramp and turned right on to the very first climb, I felt good. God, I felt good! Whoa, I'm really having to hold back here or I'll get carried away. A glance at the Garmin. Don't do too many watts and you're going to be on a good one here. Brake, corner, accelerate. Settle.

The first checkpoint, a third of the way in, a chance to see how I was performing against Chris and Roglič and Dumoulin. Faster than all of them, up too against Michał Kwiatkowski, who had set the day's fastest time so far, even though that mattered not at all for the GC. This is better than good. Nico Portal on the team radio in my ear. 'You're up, G! Keep it going, keep it steady . . .'

No rain in the air, the road surface drying. All good, until a sharp right-hander at the bottom of a little dip, and suddenly my back wheel was sliding and oh no . . .

I'm not even really sure how it happened. The corner was a little slippy, the pace was up and maybe I was on the brakes a fraction late. You either stay on board instinctively in a moment like that or you're down before you realise it. This time I held it up.

It got a little busy on the radio after that. 'Yes, you're up, you're doing well. Press on when you can but every corner just relax, just take it easy, no stress. You're up. You can afford to lose two minutes on Dumoulin and still win the Tour. So don't risk anything, right?' Dave was also in the car following behind me with Nico. I couldn't help but have a little chuckle to myself. 'God, I bet Dave's stressed now . . .' That Dauphiné prologue still on everyone's minds.

It was good to hear but also difficult to implement on the move. You can't ride a time-trial bike cautiously. I struggle to ride any bike cautiously. You lose your rhythm into corners if you're overthinking how you're going to take them, and there were still a lot more corners to come. It's like when you're in your car waiting at a set of lights about to do a hill-start and another car pulls up directly behind you. Suddenly you start overthinking it. Something you've done a thousand times before suddenly becomes difficult. In any other time trial in any other race, the reaction would have been totally different – oh yes, that happens, just keep riding hard and take it a bit more carefully into corners. But this was not an ordinary time trial. It was no ordinary race.

Up ahead, Roglič was suffering from his exertions over the Tourmalet and Aspin the day before. At the second checkpoint, twenty-two kilometres in, he was forty-nine seconds down on Froomey, which meant Chris was closing in on third place overall and a spot on the podium come Paris. I was thirteen seconds up on Chris. I was fifteen ahead of Dumoulin. I was on fire.

Think only of the corner in front of you, G. Process not outcome. Slow into every corner, real slow but trying to get the power down and ride as hard as I could in between. I had Dave's voice in my head – 'You can lose five seconds on every corner today, G, and still win . . .' Eight or nine corners to come on the final descent, so a big push up the Col de Pinodieta, knowing I must still be within a few seconds of third and second on the stage, and then taking it oh-so-slow down the other side, looking long, thinking big. Risk nothing. Get to the bottom of this and you've won it.

I ticked those final corners off. That's that one done, that's another done. Nice and easy, but also weirdly frustrating, even with that great prize awaiting me just up the road. I'm a racing cyclist. If it had been drier, I could have hammered down there. Even though it wasn't, I still wanted to. I could see the corners coming. I had the legs and the speed ... I would later find out from Tim that I had lost eleven seconds to Froomey in that one descent alone. I could have won that stage.

I wanted to, but I wanted something else even more. 500m to go, shouting into the radio mic on my chest. I wanted reassurance. After everything I had been through – the doubts, the falls, the wondering – I wanted to know beyond any doubt.

'Nico, have I won the fucking Tour?'

'G. You've won the Tour!'

A release of everything that had been held back for so long. Forget about processes. Forget about day-by-day, about not getting ahead of myself, about tactics and low-carbs and saving energy and not daring to believe. Fire the bullets. Spray the skies.

I took my hands off the bar and roared. I never go no-handed on my TT bike, especially on the road. It's dodgy.

Roaring inside an aero helmet makes even less sense. You've got a visor covering most of your face. No one can hear you, except you, very loudly.

I was in my own beautiful little world, my own little celebration. I forgot entirely that any of it was live on international television, that there might be millions of people watching. It was just me and a big celebration for myself.

Dumoulin had taken the stage. Froome was a second off, me cruising home thirteen seconds down. A GC lead of almost two minutes, a lead that could never be overtaken.

The first person I saw when I crossed the line was Sara. She was wearing a red dress, and walking down the middle of the road. No one else was in a red dress and no one else was walking down the middle of the road, so she was relatively easy to spot. We locked onto each other. Sa and I, winning the Tour de France.

We did a lot of hugging. There weren't so many words, mainly 'wow'. I was shocked she was there. She had told me she would be taking the dog for a walk, because when she takes the dog for a walk there's no phone signal, so she could cope with the tension. The real reason she had had no phone signal was because she was on a private jet laid on by Sky, all the commercial flights from Cardiff or Bristol, or anywhere close, all booked by supporters. So once 'wow' was done, a fuller thought replaced it: you cheeky little thing, it all makes sense now.

I was properly sweaty as well. I had an undervest on a day that was already muggy when you were just walking about. It must have been horrible to hug me. She must have been covered in sweat. Although I don't think she really cared at that moment.

I dumped a bottle of water over my head, so now I was wet in all the places I hadn't already been sweaty. Sorry, Sa. I attempted a first television interview, and I was as much of a mess as I had been on my wedding day. Being a bloke, you don't really think about what's actually going to happen when you get married. It's going to be good, all my mates are going to be there, my family, we're going to have a good time. That's all you think about for the wedding. You don't actually think you're going to be in a church getting married, with nieces singing, and everyone you love all smiling at you. I cried then so hard and for so long that even the vicar told me to man up.

It was the same on that damp street in a town that no one had heard of in the south-west of France. I hadn't thought about what it would be like to actually win it. Suddenly I had. Bloody hell.

Everyone was hugging and everyone was crying. Dave Brailsford went for the double hug, one arm round my neck and the other round Sa's. Dave has known me since I was a seventeen-year-old on the junior British programme. We've been through a lot together. Through that, he has felt both like a boss – sometimes a scary one – and a stepdad. In this moment he was more stepdad than boss.

My weepiness was having a similar effect on everyone else. Dave looking away. 'Fucking hell, G, don't get me started as well.' Then Tim was there, and the same thing happened to him. I loved it. Lots of men who never cry, all crying at the same time. For a happy reason.

It's a glamorous world when you win the Tour. You go to dope control and you sit there for about two hours unable to produce any wee, because you had a big one before getting on your bike and then you sweated a hell of a lot while not drinking anything. I sat there with Dan Martin, reminiscing about the old days when we had raced each other as juniors, wondering what the two of us would have said had we known where we would end up, one in yellow, one a stage winner who was just awarded the combativity prize as the rider who had done the most to animate the race. Froomey was there, and George our media officer, who hadn't wanted to say anything all the way through the three weeks in case he jinxed it. Chris and I shared another hug. His happiness and congratulations were genuine. Cheers, mate.

Winning the Tour hits you in stages. You get taken to something called the winner's press conference. I had a moment walking in when I thought, whoa, that's me, isn't it? You go back to your hotel and the chef has done burgers and chips, albeit highly nutritious burgers and excellent chips. You have a beer, and you fancy about a thousand more, and then you remember you do actually have to finish Sunday's stage in Paris, and you park that thought for another twenty-four hours.

I couldn't sleep that night until almost 3 a.m. I was buzzing, my phone was buzzing. So many messages, and I wanted to reply to every one. I felt like I should. You win the Tour and you're shattered but because you've won the

Tour, you're too excited to sleep. That's the hard stuff to anticipate.

I was brushing my teeth, looking in the mirror, when another wave hit me. I've actually done it. I started laughing at my own reflection, baggy eyes, foaming mouth. Bloody hell. I've won the Tour!

Sara Thomas

I don't know if people believed Ger when he said he was just taking it day by day, but we were, we genuinely were. I'd found it so hard to watch the critical stages. The descent on stage 19 had been awful. My dad couldn't stand it in the house and went out. My mum couldn't bear to watch either. We couldn't put the television coverage on. You try not to think about it or talk about it, but it's all you can think about. There's no conversation.

We ended up sitting on my mum's bed. Mum had a shower for something to do. Then we watched *Tenable*, the game show on ITV with Warwick Davis, just to burn through more time. Not speaking much, half-watching, half-thinking, God, is he alright? Relying on updates from Fran Millar and Luke's wife, Cath, their messages getting more fraught with every kilometre that passed. Then the sheer relief of that text that said, 'He's crossed the line, it's all fine . . .'

He had no idea I'd be there at the finish of the time trial. And my first thought, when he hugged me, was – blimey, you are so sweaty. I knew he'd be emotional; it was exactly like our wedding. At your wedding, it just hits you. When you don't let yourself think about something, then all of a sudden it happens in a rush.

I'd been there for all the Team Sky wins apart from Bradley's. They were all obviously special, all a bit different. This one, there was a different kind of feeling with everyone. Rod was crying and Dave was crying. Tim doesn't cry. Tim is only interested in crying if he can use it to measure someone's hydration levels. Oh my God, Tim's welling up! And that set me off. Seeing how much it meant to other people made it even more special.

For me, there were three main emotions swirling around. Part of me was in shock: these things don't happen. I always believed Geraint was capable, but to go twenty-one consecutive days without a major incident was unbelievable.

Relief. The relief I felt was immense. The knot that had been building in my stomach had finally been released, the weight had lifted and I could breathe knowing I didn't have to worry about tomorrow. Relief that he was no longer the nearly man, that it wasn't another year gone without reward for all the hard work gone into it. Relief that after all this time, it had finally gone right.

And joy. Pure joy. I'd seen everything that went into this win, and if this was the pay-off for all those setbacks and heartbreaks, it was so worth it. I'd watched my husband achieve his biggest dream, a dream that had felt so far away so many times. The happiness I felt was beyond measure.

The bridesmaid finally got his massive white wedding.

Chapter Sixteen

Drop the Mic

I barely slept. Honestly. If I hadn't had a yellow jersey to wear on the Champs-Élysées I would have had breakfast and gone back to bed. It was that sort of weariness. I've done it! I haven't quite done it. I've got 116km left to cycle, first through some average outer suburbs of Paris and then rapidly up and down the slap-bam middle.

We also had a flight to catch. From Biarritz to Paris, a load of tired cyclists, all on the same plane, all looking forward to going home. At least on this one they treated us to some proper in-flight food. There was some sort of pretzel bread that tasted, after so long on the straight and narrow, lovely and salty. A big day, small pleasures.

It was still hard to take it all in. The stage was still a stage. I didn't want to puncture or crash. The sprinters would be racing hard at the front, so I would still have to be switched on, but I wanted to enjoy it too. It was a strange sort of Tour limbo: the winner, but not yet won; celebrated, but not yet celebrating.

The support was extraordinary. Half of Wales seemed to be heading for Paris, many of them related to me. Sa was there, with her mum Beth, dad Eif, and brother Rhys, plus her uncle, godfather and family friends. My mum and dad came, and my brother and his girlfriend. My uncle, auntie and two cousins and their partners. My best man and his wife, plus two good mates who were ushers at my wedding. A big gang of Luke Rowe's Cardiff mates, my agent Luke. Some with tickets, some in hospitality, others just sprinkled all over the city. One notable absence was my sister-in-law, Carys. She had said she was unable to make it on account of being thirty-six weeks pregnant, but part of me will always think she was boycotting it as she thought she'd be the one getting all the family attention that summer. Carys?

I'd loved watching the final stage of the Tour as a kid. For all the happy clichés across the first three weeks – the schoolkids *en masse* in uniform by the side of the road, the helicopter shots of snowy mountain peaks, a chateau straight from a fairy-tale – there was one Parisian moment that I always loved: the shot of the riders emerging from the tunnel, the camera on the long boom swinging to track their progress. It had blown my mind as a twenty-one-year-old limping towards the finish line, more so than seeing the Eiffel Tower as we rolled towards the city, or curving up past the Arc de Triomphe. I'm here, I'm part of it. I've arrived.

And now I was at the weird centre of all of it, riding a yellow bike with yellow handlebar tape, ticking off the clichés I'd watched Chris Froome enjoy but barely dared dream might involve me: riding along for the first few kilometres outside Houilles with a glass of champagne in my hand; toasting teammates, toasting a grinning Dave Brailsford leaning out of the car; being handed a Welsh flag, trying to unfurl it and let it flutter behind me while also not riding into the gutter. It's harder than you think, especially after a glass of champagne.

It was surreal. That first fifty kilometres is something of a slog. You just want to start the nine laps of the Champs-Élysées. Drink-riding is all very well but it gets to a point where you start thinking, can we not just get there now and properly enjoy it and have a good party?

Riders were coming alongside to offer a pat on the back or a word of congratulations. Riders you'd expect, like Daryl Impey, an old mate, and Greg Van Avermaet, as well as relatively random French and Spanish guys. A thumbs up as they rolled past, a shout and a smile. Daniele Bennati, the veteran Italian who had been part of Mario Cipollini's lead-out train many years before. 'Hi, it was really good to see you win. It gives me goosebumps!' I laughed, assuming he was joking, because I had never been on the same team as him and came from a different cycling culture, although he was someone I'd always watched and looked up to. His face went serious. 'No no,' he said, and pointed at his arm. Goosebumps.

It can feel heavy going at times riding up the Champs-Élysées. It's steeper and longer than it looks. It's not the Mûr-de-Bretagne, but in the same way that on the Mûr you always think that you're at the top when you're not, so this road seems to stretch on forever. Maybe it's the size of the Arc de Triomphe that fools the eye. It's so big that even when you're a mile away it looks as if it must be within 200m.

This afternoon it felt easy. I don't know whether it was the giddy buzz of being almost entirely dressed in yellow, or the slight headwind down the home straight that pushed at our backs as we rode the other way down the hill, but the laps were flying by quickly. There were Union flags and Welsh dragons and familiar shouts and cheers in all directions. I almost felt as if I were floating.

Maybe it was because I didn't drink the night before. I'm glad I had a clear head to appreciate the atmosphere, the insane support, the noise and the colour. On your wedding day, you feel that it's going by so fast that you want to press pause just to take it all in. Here I was, stuck in the middle of wanting to enjoy this extraordinary ride and soak it all up, but at the same time wanting to celebrate with all my friends and family and the team.

The sprinters did their thing. I could see Arnaud Démare being put in position by FDJ, John Degenkolb hunting a second stage win for Trek, Alexander Kristoff moving up through the line. I looked around for my teammates, ready to tick off another box on Champs-Élysées bingo, the photo of the team, arms on each other's shoulders, crossing the line, but Michał Kwiatkowski had punctured on the last lap, and instead it was just me and Froomey.

That worked, even if it was still weird that he was in the ordinary white Sky jersey and I was in yellow, the reverse of the way we had ridden this famous circuit so many times. An arm round each other, big grins, Chris with the veteran's advice. 'Congratulations, G. Enjoy every second of it.'

Up to the line. From the streets of suburban Cardiff to the centre of Paris, wearing the yellow jersey. My journey was complete.

It was a totally different feeling to the day before. After the time trial it was all about the massive release of emotion, about finally being able to enjoy the moment, about not having to stay focused and think about the next day. It was an unbelievable high. Crossing the finish line in Paris was incredible but didn't trigger the same liberation. I'd had time to think about it; I'd been champion-elect for twenty-four hours. In place of the raw emotion, something equally special: seeing the Champs-Élysées lined with Welsh and British flags, knowing that out in the crowd were so many of the people who meant the most to me. I was able to take it all in.

And it was mayhem. Waiting for Kwiato, when he was taking forever to get his own personal lap of honour done, trying to get that picture taken while being stampeded by photographers. Sara and Fran Millar almost getting trampled, one losing a shoe, the other getting an elbow in the face.

I'm still not quite sure where my podium speech came from. Just before I went up, Sa and Fran egged me on to do a mic drop. I can't, I still haven't worked out what I'm going to say . . .

I'd seen Froomey give speeches in previous wins. I'd always been half-cut by then. It seemed so easy. Now my head appeared to be on a different planet. I didn't want to start mentioning people other than teammates, because that's a slippery slope and you leave someone out who has done loads for you and is thus mortally offended. And then I began, draped in the Welsh flag, and I couldn't even get their names out.

'I've not got a good track record with speeches, so I'll keep it short.

'I just want to say thanks to the team. It's just been incredible, the whole week. Obviously the riders – Luke Rowe, erm, Egan Bernal. Castroviejo. Er, I'm going to forget them now . . .'

A glance to my left, at the man standing alongside me on the podium. 'Froomey! Big respect to Froomey. Obviously it could have got awkward, it could have got tense, but mate, you were a great champion, I'll always have respect for you. Thanks a lot.'

Applause. A blank mind.

'Who else is on the team? Oh yeah – Wout. Wouter Lambertus Martinus Henricus Poels. That's his name. His proper name.

'Er. Gianni Moscon. That's six. Who am I forgetting now?'

A tap on the shoulder from Tom Dumoulin on my other side, a quick whisper.

'Oh, Kwiato! Thanks, mate. It's just . . . I'm pretty tired. The whole team was incredible, the staff as well, everyone.

'And yeah. I got into cycling because of this race. I remember running home from school to watch the end of the Tour de France, and the dream was always just to be a part of it. That came true twelve years ago, back in 2007.'

Brief pause to redo the maths.

'Now I'm here, stood in the yellow jersey. It's insane, it's incredible, it's a dream come true. Massive respect to Tom, as well, and all my rivals – it was a great race.'

More applause.

'I just want to say a final thanks to everyone out there. To the crowd, you've just been amazing. All the support I've got. Oh, my wife! I forgot my wife!'

Laughter. Sympathetic, mocking, you decide.

'Obviously a big thanks to Sara. Without you, I wouldn't be stood here. The support through thick and thin, obviously the down times. And that's the big thing to everyone back home: kids at Maindy Flyers, just dream big. If people tell you it can't be done, just believe in yourself and work hard. Keep going. You're going to have knocks, you're going to have downs, but keep believing. Anything is possible. With hard work, everything pays off in the end.

'Again, thanks for all the support – you've been amazing, we all appreciate it. Thank you very much.'

Pause.

'Vive la Tour!'

Mic drop.

Well, I thought I might as well drop it. And I think I just about managed to salvage the speech. At least it was me. I wasn't trying to be anyone else. I still couldn't believe I was on the top step of the podium; it had felt so surreal looking out beyond the photographers at what from my perspective was a mainly empty Champs-Élysées. I'd wanted to have both a Welsh flag and a Union flag on the podium, but I hadn't been prepared. Taking two separate flags would have been awkward and looked messy; I needed to spend some time somewhere connecting them together so I could drape one big flag over my shoulders. Even the Welsh one had been grabbed from one of the fans on the side of the road. There would also be no winner's cheque to be handed over, not until well into the next year. That's how it works at the Tour. I would also split it – fifteen per cent to the staff, the rest divided equally between the riders. You don't win the Tour on your own, and so you don't enjoy the spoils on your own either.

Then back to more media duties, and it appeared it wasn't just the riders who were happy it was over. Speaking to the press – the S4C crew, Gareth Rhys Owen from the BBC, Matt Rendell and Matt Stephens at the finish line – was totally different to how it had been the last week and a half. The previous days it had been a lot more serious. Now it felt like a chat with my mates. Impartiality had gone out the window and they seemed just as happy as some of the fans on the side of the road. Those guys become part of your daily routine during the Tour. They were inside my race bubble, and you form a weird bond. You don't get to know them because the conversation is heavily one-sided, but seeing them at the finish line feels like seeing friends. They were part of this race with me.

The walk back to the bus was long, over a kilometre flanked by ten bodyguards dressed head to toe in Vittel uniform. A few weird moments with practical implications. A few people spotted me and saw an opportunity to get a quick photo, but they were forced to take it from a distance since the bodyguards were clearly in more of a rush to get home than I was.

We happened to walk past Rhys, Sa's brother, who started

to initiate a hug but then thought better of it after seeing the body language of the Vittel army.

'You know what, Ger, I'll just see you later.'

'Nah, sod it. Come here . . .'

I also learned that were Sa a rider, she wouldn't make it through the first week of the Tour without losing an hour. She can't hold her position in a group. She was repeatedly spat out the back of the mini Vittel peloton, and the team doctor had to drop back and pace her back each time. She can't use size as an excuse, Egan had done alright.

Time for a brief reflection. I always thought I could win the Tour, but never the way I just had. On four of the six big mountain days in the Alps and Pyrenees, I took time out of my rivals. The two I didn't were the long, downhill finishes where there was a breakaway. I took time out of Tom Dumoulin, my closest rival, on seven stages. Not until the time trial did he do that to me, and I reckoned I could have won that too had I not been playing it safe. I'm still annoyed about the time trial, if I'm honest.

None of it mattered now, but I thought I could maybe have won on the Col du Portet. If Egan had ridden for me rather than dropping back to help Chris, and we'd gone all in for the stage, we might have bridged across to Dan Martin and then Quintana. If we had gone for the stage, I had the legs to do it. Had Dumoulin not lost Primož Roglič's wheel on the descent on stage 20, I might have won that too. Maybe that was being greedy, but when you looked back it was crazy.

I remembered going out for food with Sa when the route

had been announced, all those months ago. There are only three proper summit finishes, Sa, that's good for me. During the race, people were looking at the next big mountain stage and saying, this will be the one he cracks on. And we were all looking at it entirely the wrong way round. Every time the mountains came, I was the strongest.

There had been digs from some that it was remarkable how a former track rider could now ride like this in the hills. It was one of those partial truths that ultimately turned out to be meaningless. I'd won Olympic gold on the track, but in an endurance event. I wasn't Chris Hoy or Jason Kenny. Track riding had given me the time-trialling skills and the mental strength to take the opportunity in France that otherwise may have slipped away. And I'd been a road rider long before, winning junior Paris–Roubaix. I grew up riding road.

I was a cyclist, and I loved riding my bike. I had trained for a four-minute race under a roof and I had trained for five-hour road stages out in the wind and hail. Why categorise me? All of my life, my obsessions, my riding, had been leading to now. The only remarkable thing had been the lack of doubts and dramas.

I had been in control for three weeks. Now it was time to let the brakes off. Messily.

Dave Brailsford

Principal, Team Sky

I left Wales when I was eighteen. Thirty-odd years in cycling, but it's always been my home, and my whole journey in cycling, all the emotions I've experienced on the way, are related to my Welsh roots, to my very core. I understood what Geraint's win meant: for him, for me, for the team, and for Wales, too, for my friends and family. Somehow that seemed to bubble up inside me, mixed with an immense sense of pride for Geraint himself. A national hero, and also the epitome of making the sacrifices, of doing the hard yards, of being tenacious but also of making all that pay off, of not being scared of holding your hand up when you get an opportunity. He's brave in that sense. He's not scared of the failure of it.

We'd seen him have so many crashes and setbacks over the years. I remember the Giro, the Tour in 2017, the Olympics road race. I remember when he had his accident over in Australia and ruptured his spleen, and we had to fly his parents out. I remember all of the worry and the concern about that. I remember him riding as the youngest team member in the World Championships in the team pursuit.

I remember him getting drunk with Ed Clancy and all the young lads when they were on the Academy, when they went running out of a hotel and I had to chase them round a field.

It's a funny thing. You hold all those emotions in. I always do. But every now and again something happens which triggers that release, and that's what happened to me. I was so immensely proud of him and happy and all the rest of it. The experience was way, way bigger than winning a bike race, if that makes sense.

The closer you get to a victory and the more important it is, the more people start to think about how much they have to lose, and how awful it would be if they did. It's so hard to manage all those emotions and keep them to one side, to stay as the assassin, cold and calculated, making great decisions, being a little bit ruthless. It's where in sport you quite often see people, having got so close, falling by the wayside.

One of the remarkable observations about Geraint was how he kept it together throughout the whole race. He came in calm and very focused at the start of the race and he kept that focus, despite all of the challenges and the noise and the crowd and the intensity of it all. There were more potential distractions than I've ever experienced in any other race, yet he didn't engage with any of them. That mentality had been years and years in the making. Had he been twenty-six or twenty-seven, with the same form and the same physical condition, he'd have found it a lot harder to win that race.

People kept coming up to me and saying, can he see it through? He's going to have a bad day, isn't he? But when you actually look at it, there was absolutely no reason whatsoever why he would capitulate at any point. He had ridden a brilliant race; he'd been protected the whole race. He was the most efficient rider across the three weeks; the way he'd managed his energy level, his efforts on the bike, his fuelling and nutrition and hydration on and off the bike – it was second to none. There was absolutely no reason why all of a sudden, out the blue, his body and mind would fail.

I followed him in the car on that final time trial. You could see straight away that he was strong, that he was on it, that staying on the bike was probably the greatest challenge of the day. And he had that one little slip in the corner, when he completely lost the front wheel, and my heart stopped, and I got a horrible taste in the back of my throat, and I thought, oh Jesus . . . But then he held it up and I thought right, this is his day. If he's held that up, nothing is going to happen. It's going to be okay. It's his race now, it's meant to be.

I was never surprised. I think I always believed he could win the Tour. It was piecing together the performance rather than his ability to win the race. I think there's a difference in that; a lot of people have got ability to do amazing things but they just can't put it all together. You can look round the peloton and you can identify riders with immense talent, but they just don't seem to be able to do it all under pressure when it really matters, over that duration of riding. I think that was the challenge that he overcame. And it was brilliant, an absolute highlight of my career, no doubt about it.

Chapter Seventeen

The Boy Who Climbed A Mountain

There were beers waiting for us on the bus. Lovely, cold beers. The first one went down so fast it was almost as if it had evaporated. The second followed the first at pace. Luke started a song. We all joined in. There were so many people on the bus I didn't recognise them all, which made sense when I asked one bloke who he was and realised from his half-arsed answer that he was no one to do with anything. 'Good blagging, mate, now off you jump.'

Rod Ellingworth had tears running down his face. It almost got me going again. I had already seen my dad shed a little tear when he was being interviewed by S4C. To see people close to you, who you had never seen emotional before, getting emotional for something you've done was both weird and wonderful. Rod had been my coach since I was eighteen. He had been my cycling father figure, teaching me how to compete on the road and how to behave off it, testing me and guiding my response. He had seen one of his original posse, Mark Cavendish, win the world road race championship back in Copenhagen in 2011. Now it was another Rod graduate taking the Tour.

Everything goes fast-forward on a night like that. The bus took us back to the hotel. Every year we relished this little interlude, all the riders and their partners, the key staff and Nico Portal's children, the cutest kids in the world. It's the only time where it's just us, the team that's been on the road together for almost four weeks, celebrating together before we get off and are pulled in separate directions. The adrenaline is still pumping so tiredness isn't an issue. The beers are flowing and music blaring, Oasis, Robbie Williams, and in the last few years, 'You'll Never Walk Alone', courtesy of nutritionist James Morton, aka Murph, formerly of Liverpool FC. Plus another recent tradition: multiple marriage proposals from Wout to his girlfriend, Alice.

Almost too soon we are back at the hotel. The fastest shower in the world, the annual discussion with Sa. No, you haven't got time to wash your hair. No, that dress is fine, it's not too creased, let's go.

There was proper partying to be done. We headed to a bar that Sky had booked for us. Fortunately, they had learned the lessons of previous years and gone for somewhere cosy rather than barn-like, and with proper food – pizzas, burgers, chips – rather than the vol-au-vents and amuse-bouches that were served up one year. Imagine riding a complete lap of France, thrashing yourself into oblivion day after day for three weeks, watching every single mouthful of food that passes your lips, and then at the end of it all someone offers you a cracker the size of a two-pence piece with a shaving of smoked salmon on top.

Everyone was there who should have been there. Sa. My

parents. My brother. My in-laws. My mates. The team. Dave. Rod. It quickly took on the feeling of a messy wedding. You wanted to talk to everyone, but there were so many people you loved that you felt like you only had an unsatisfactory three minutes with each. I had to do another speech, this one a little spicier than the original one of the Champs-Élysées. I was honest in all the topics I decided to touch upon, let's put it that way.

I also mentioned that when I crossed the finish line, I had realised that I would have to pay all the boys in the team a bonus, just as Brad Wiggins had done in 2012, just as Froomey had done multiple times. Then I pointed out that I only actually had to pay them for three days. 'No, mate,' Luke shouted out, 'it's three weeks . . .' Nope, you lot only decided to ride for me for the last three days of the entire thing. So I'll work out the usual bonus, divide it into twenty-one stages, and you can have three portions of that. Split seven ways.

At your wedding, you get a sense throughout that you've spent so much time dreaming about the day that when it finally arrives, it all goes by too fast. You don't want it to end, but it's just bang, bang, bang. And even as it's flying past, you know that every moment is special, and you'll never have that exact group of people together ever again. That's what winning the Tour feels like.

At a wedding, you have that point where you look around the dance floor and half the men have taken their ties off and tied them round their heads. That night I looked around and half the men had their shirts off. Luke Rowe. My dad.

Fashion designer Jeff Banks, who was there because he loves his cycling and very kindly sorted me out with the suits for my actual wedding. Dave Brailsford, which no one expected. Dave barely drinks any more because he's so full-on with his training and diet, so when he decided to get stuck in, he was absolutely flying.

At one point Dave came roaring over to me.

'G! We're all taking our shirts off! Take your shirt off, G!'

'Ah, Dave, you're alright.'

You don't argue with Dave at the best of times, and certainly not when he's got his shirt off and five continental lagers down his neck. Before I could twitch, he had grabbed my shirt front and ripped it open. Buttons everywhere, buttons bouncing about on the floor. Sa was gobsmacked. 'Ger, I liked that shirt! Your brother Alun got you that for Christmas.' Luckily, my brother was at a similar level to Dave and had no idea. He wouldn't have noticed had a button flown off and hit him in the eye.

It wasn't the most attractive of sights. Riders at the end of a Tour have upper bodies with all the muscular definition of thirteen-year-old girls. We are also deathly pale except for our forearms, which look like they've been treated with Ronseal. So too do our faces, except for the white Y-shaped stripes where our helmet straps have been, and the panda eyes left by our sunglasses. My dad is in his sixties. Dave was all over the shop. Jeff Banks was probably in the best shape. Jeff Banks looks after himself. And he has a magnificent unbroken tan.

Jeff also had a present for me. It must be quite hard to get something for someone who's just won the Tour de France. I certainly didn't expect a cigar, but I am almost certain it was an expensive one, because that's how Jeff rolls. I'm not a world-leading expert in cigars.

The bar had a proper dance floor. It also came with a DJ who was a little too cool for school. His tunes of choice may have been cutting-edge but we needed wedding classics. Luke and I went over and made a few requests. He responded, and so did the guests. Within minutes, an empty dance floor had been transformed into a seething mass of shirtless men and their slightly wary partners.

Apparently we got in about 5 a.m. I have that on authority from Sa, because there is no way I can independently verify it. On big nights you can sometimes struggle to sleep because you're too wired. Your body is desperate for rest but another part is keen to party on. I woke about 10.30 a.m., nowhere near as hungry as I should have been, which suggested I'd done significantly more damage to the burgers and chips than I remembered. My phone was going crazy with messages. The priority was to check if I'd posted anything humiliating on social media. I was in the main okay, although I was shocked to see an Instagram story I had posted of Sa and I eating a Welsh cake in bed had made the front page of the *Evening Standard*. Then I saw a message I'd sent to Daryl Impey: 'Tucking terrify Henry'. Possibly a reference to an unexpected video message of congratulations I'd received from Thierry Henry. That apart, all was good. I had offended neither a person nor a nation.

After five hours' sleep and nine hours of celebrating, the

last thing you want is the check-in mayhem and security queue horrors of Charles de Gaulle international airport. I've experienced them in the past after Tours have finished, and they are almost enough to break you at that stage. The fact that Sky laid on a private jet to take us all back to London was thus a thing of beauty. Straight to the secret Other Terminal, sit there for ten minutes and then straight on the plane. I'm a man more familiar with EasyJet. I relished every second.

We were taken straight from Farnborough to Sky HQ in Isleworth. There was a Welsh male choir to welcome us and a phalanx from Maindy Flyers. My brain was so slow at processing what I wanted to say, so weary and hungover, that it took me a while to get back in the groove of doing interviews. Shuttled directly on to the BBC for *The One Show*, I thought: this could go either way. I could successfully fly this by the seat of my pants, or I could be really bad and not be able to speak, especially as it's live. The presenters were my compatriot Alex Jones and the man I had previously referred to as the *Countryfile* dude, Matt Baker. I'll now forever remember him fondly, since one of the guys working on the show let me have a kip in his special dressing room. Twenty minutes of power-napping followed by a coffee later, I was a man reborn.

If a day with a private jet is a good one, a day with a private jet that ends with a suite in the Dorchester is almost too much for a kid from Cardiff. I still don't actually know where in London the Dorchester is. It may as well have been another planet. When I walked into the room – the rooms – there was a display of little cakes and truffles, each with a different picture of me from the Tour on top. There were also two bottles of champagne. I ordered steak and chips from room service and learned something new: at the Dorchester, steak and chips off room service is seventy pounds. Still, I reasoned, if they're happy to stick me in a suite, what's an extra seventy quid on top? So I ordered the chocolate fondant for pudding, too.

It was the first moment since crossing the finish line in Paris that it was just me and Sa. Just like our wedding day again. That night I really did struggle to sleep. The buzz was kicking in, even if I had to keep reminding myself what had just happened. Man, I won the Tour de France! It gave me a chance to start replying to all those messages. I wanted to reply to each one. Everyone who had sent something was part of my life in some small but significant way. I wanted to share with them everything I was feeling.

There should be rest when you win the Tour, but there isn't. Up at 7 a.m. to do Radio 4's *Today* programme at 7.30 a.m., then a spruce-up to do the BBC *Breakfast* show shortly afterwards. Interviews with newspapers and magazines and television crews for the next five hours, and then another private jet to a criterium in Holland. Criteriums – circuit races around big city centres – are a staple of the post-Tour scene. The organisers pay the stars of the past month good money to entertain their fans, and the stars respond by putting on a good show. A break from some, Luke steering me through, not least when we heard it would total eighty kilometres – a drop in the Tour ocean, but forever after the forty-eight hours I'd had. Me, Tom Dumoulin and Bauke Mollema went clear with three laps to go, me winning the sprint from Tom.

The next morning I was back on EasyJet, heading home to Monaco. Back to reality, back to sitting on the runway for two hours before it took off. I was destroyed. Everything I had been through piled up on top of me in those hours – the emotional release, the beers, the delayed exhaustion. You might have a yellow jersey in your carry-on, but you also have your knees up by your ears and the three-year-old on the row behind repeatedly opening and shutting his tray table onto your shoulder blades.

I barely moved off the sofa the following day. Even sending messages from my phone drew a heavy sigh of fatigue. Luke called to see if I fancied a ride. I was honest with him, and met him in a wine bar afterwards instead. My lethargy had extended to the kitchen, which was fine at the time but less so later when the bottles started piling up on the table in front of us and I remembered that I hadn't eaten since the scrambled eggs at breakfast.

Sara knows what I'm like on these sort of occasions. She and some of the girls joined us after a few hours. 'Oh dear, Ger. This is going to be one of those nights, isn't it?'

Yes. Yes, it is. They bring you nibbles in wine bars, small cubes of ham and cheese, but they're never sufficient to soak up what else has been consumed. We then moved on to the same bar where I had drunk George North to sleep the year before. It was happy hour, which was good news for the wallet but bad news for the skinny cyclist. It also lasted for two hours, which had the same two knock-on effects.

At some point we went for a steak while the girls left us to it. I know this because I later saw a video I posted on the family WhatsApp group, which in retrospect I was glad I didn't also post on social media. My phone battery went at some point, so I was texting Sa from Luke's mobile. At 3 a.m. I told her I was leaving for home, a journey that usually takes fifteen minutes. Half an hour passed. Luke had got home. Sa was calling his wife, Cath. So Luke's back, where's Geraint? There had been stories in the local media about a British tourist who had had an accident in the city recently, fallen down something and died. In Sa's head I became that tourist, and so she went out looking for me – except somehow, as she was leaving the block of flats, I managed to get in, even though I didn't have a key. Possibly the concierge did me a favour. Maybe I tailgated a fellow resident. Either way she was running around the streets of Monaco at 3 a.m. while I was sleeping happily on the mat outside our front door. When she eventually returned, stepping out of the lift to see a familiar set of legs sticking out from around the corner, she says she was almost as happy as on the Champs-Élysées. And then immediately very angry, and justifiably so.

It was a pattern that continued for the next few days. Sara on a hen-do, Richie Porte organising a meal, Luke and I going along and then kicking on. All I can say is there was an awful lot of pent-up fun that needed to escape. Barely a single drink for nine months, every night an early one, every meal much smaller than one would ideally like. It's going to have an effect in the end.

Strange things continued to happen. I got an email and video message from Elton John. I was handed a phone by Sky's Fran Millar with a call in progress from someone called Arsène. I answered it, heard a French voice and assumed it was Bradley Wiggins doing one of his excellent impersonations. To be told by Mr Wenger that he had been watching me at the Tour, that he had been impressed by what he saw, was the equivalent for me of being handed an Arsenal shirt with my name on it and running out at the Emirates. Which would also happen, about a fortnight later. Madness, all of it. Arsène may of course have been making it up; I didn't push him. 'Right, so what was the name of the summit finish where I came past Mikel Nieve in the last 500m? Who pulled a big turn on the first eight kilometres of Alpe d'Huez once Kwiato dropped back?'

The video messages kept coming. There was the one from Thierry Henry the night of the after-party, being so Thierry Henry. 'Wow. Geraint Thomas! Crossing the line on the Champs-Élysées in the yellow jersey. I watched some of the *étapes*, as we say in France. Wow!' Messages from All Black legend Dan Carter, from former Wales and Lions captain Sam Warburton. One from the actor Michael Sheen, proud Welshman, decent footballer too. My agent had gone through Kate Beckinsale to get that one, for some reason not stopping at Kate Beckinsale along the way. Seemingly all the greatest names in Welsh sport – Colin Jackson, Ryan Giggs, Mark Hughes, George North. Gareth Bale, along with Sam and me that other sporting graduate of Whitchurch High School. The idea that Giggsy and Henry actually knew who I might be was impossible for me to get my head around. So was talk that I might be nominated for BBC Sports Personality of the Year. What, alongside Harry Kane and Anthony Joshua? I couldn't comprehend it.

I hadn't made all the sacrifices down the years, all the training, for this aftermath. I'd done it because I wanted to win the greatest race of all. And yet I realised a stone had been dropped in a far larger pool than I could have imagined. It was the messages from complete strangers that meant as much as anything; a tweet from someone saying my boy wanted to ride his bike today for the first time because of you, a video sent by a ten-year-old girl of her riding Mont Ventoux, telling me she was my biggest fan, then clarifying it in the way that a ten-year-old does and saying, well, probably one of the biggest. It made me think back to what I was like at the same age, the people I looked up to then. To think kids might be doing that to me was as satisfying as all the rest of it.

I was back in Cardiff early the following week. The city had arranged a homecoming parade for me, starting down at the Senedd, the Welsh Parliament building in Cardiff Bay, working its way up through the city centre on St Mary Street and finishing outside the castle. I was convinced no one would turn up. I had no real idea what had been going on in Wales as the race bubbled to a crescendo, only a vague notion of how widely my win had been noticed. I didn't know that all the news bulletins had been leading on it that final Sunday, that the woman who had founded Maindy Flyers, Debbie Wharton, had become one of the most frequently quoted women in the country. I even had a dream on the Wednesday night that the audience was patchy when I walked onto the stage, and that as I started my speech they began drifting away, bored and uninterested, complaining about the road closures.

Sa tried to make me feel better. Don't worry, there's me and my parents and your family, and quite a few of your mates and my mates. We can just run up St Mary Street in a constant relay, so that you've always got someone alongside you as you cycle along.

It wasn't until I stepped out on the stage down in the Bay that I realised I might be okay. It was like walking out as a lead singer at Glastonbury. Faces and smiles and waving arms as far as I could see, songs going up, banners and flags and an awful lot of yellow. I was astonished. There was a welcome speech from the First Minister, Carwyn Jones, followed by a slightly more bashful thank you one from me. A procession into town with young riders from Welsh Cycling as my outriders, the crowds five or six deep on either side, up to the castle and even more spread out behind the barriers along Castle Street there. Gethin Jones on the stage to compere it all, a few more dazed, self-conscious words from me in the late afternoon sun and warm breeze: 'I'll be honest, I thought it might just be my wife and my dog . . .'

Max Boyce was there. Of course Max Boyce was there. He had written a special poem to mark the occasion, 'The

Boy Who Climbed A Mountain', and he took over at the lectern to deliver it:

Here's to Geraint Thomas, who rode and took his chance
The boy who climbed a mountain and won the Tour de France.

There's a pillar box in Cardiff, where the mayor has arranged
To buy some tins of yellow paint, and have the colour changed
And down in Cardiff City Hall, I heard the council say
We'll change the name of the Severn Bridge to the Geraint
    Thomas Way.

Now Whitchurch High are rightly proud, and love to tell the tale
How he carved his name in the wood of a desk, like Warburton
    and Bale
And where his yellow jersey hangs, beside the wooden beams
'The boy who climbed a mountain,' and dared to chase his dreams.

But there were some who doubted. 'He doesn't stand a chance!'
There's never been a Welshman who's won the Tour de France
But he's more than just a *domestique*, I've known it all along
The boy deserves a knighthood and his bike deserves a gong.

That day we'll long remember, and I'll oft recall that night
When the Senedd and the castle walls were bathed in yellow light
And I saw the round moon smiling from on its jealous height
And turn its face to yellow in the dark of Cardiff's night.

And I hope he'll make a fortune, and saves up for a yacht
And buys a second home in France, and a *pied-a-terre* in Splott
But I know that fame won't change him, and to me that's such a joy
'Cos though he lives in Monaco, he's still a Cardiff boy.

Now the Grogg shop up in Ponty are working night and day
But people are complaining there's such a long delay
The kilns are full of Geraints with a Welsh flag shouldered high
But people have to understand his hair takes time to dry.

So I hope it's fine next Thursday to welcome Geraint home
They say the Pope is coming on Easy Jet from Rome
And Donald Trump is coming too, he said it should be fun
He's flying into Cardiff and he'll be on Air Force One.

I hope it's fine on Thursday, though I think it's still in doubt
So Derek has suggested that we keep our brollies out
So I'll stand outside the City Hall, with its gilded marble dome
And sing like England football fans that 'Geraint's coming home'.

So I'll buy a Grogg of Geraint, although they don't come cheap
And I'll sell my one of Elvis, and one of Lynn the Leap
'Cos when G rode through Paris, and waved to all the crowd
He more than climbed a mountain, he made a nation proud.

Months on, I'm still not sure it's all become real for me. Each time someone says to me – 'Hey, you won the Tour de France!' – it hits me afresh. Oh yeah. I did. I won the Tour de France!

No crashes this time. The crashes were for others. No being wiped out, no separated joints, no grated skin. No ambulance, no early departure, no watching someone else achieve all they ever wanted while I struggled to get off my sofa.

I knew I was just the tip of the pyramid. You win the Tour de France through the most intense dedication and privation, but you do so in the slipstream of others. Sara. My parents. Sa's parents. Rod Ellingworth, Tim Kerrison, Dave Brailsford. Darren Tudor. My mates from Cardiff. My former teammates. The current ones. Luke Rowe, Egan Bernal, Wout Poels. Michał Kwiatkowski, Jonathan Castroviejo, Gianni Moscon. Chris Froome.

I kept the belief, even when some of the critics doubted. I always knew I could beat those riders, but to do so consistently across three weeks, on the biggest stage of all? I hoped, and I knew it could be done, and I did everything I could in training and at home to make it possible.

The support I have enjoyed on the roadside and back in Britain and on social media has been the most wonderful gift. I am grateful for every Welsh and British flag I saw fluttering against that blue July sky in France, for every yell of encouragement my ears caught as I battled up the Tourmalet and La Rosière and the Col du Portet. All those familiar faces in Paris, all the banners and face-painting, all the flights booked, trains jumped on and cars filled with petrol and brought across the Channel. It's the strongest tailwind any cyclist could hope to have.

I'm the kid who dreamed about the Tour but imagined

it as an impossible world. I'm the boy who rode up little Caerphilly Mountain outside Cardiff and pretended I was riding away from the pursuing pack on Alpe d'Huez. I started on a cheap mountain bike called the Wolf that had a little speaker on the handlebars that could make police siren and fire engine noises, and I ended on the Champs-Élysées on a carbon-fibre wonder painted yellow. I rode towards places like Cowbridge and Merthyr with jam sandwiches in my back pockets, freezing on winter mornings and being so exhausted when I got home that I had to press the doorbell with my forehead, and I celebrated in Paris with champagne in glass flutes. As well as with Jeff Banks with his shirt off and his tan on display, but still.

No more the nearly man. No more the rider who could do everything except hold on to the biggest prizes of all. No more talk of cracking in the third week, and no more giving my all just in the service of someone else. It happened, eventually. One year, one race, I showed them.

A lot about me stayed the same in 2018. But something changed, too. The boy who climbed a mountain climbed to the top of the world. And it was all yellow.

It's not the end, either. The air at the top of the mountain is thin, but it's sweet as well. I'd like to go back. Who's coming along?

Chris Froome

**Four-time Tour de France champion, winner
of the Giro d'Italia and Vuelta a España**

've always felt that the Tour de France is a race of truth.
There's no hiding when you get in to the high mountains. Ultimately the strongest rider should win the world's
biggest bike race, but that's often not the case. There is
always the possibility of external factors outside of your
control changing the course of your race in a second, and
Geraint knows that all too well. This year G was the strongest
rider, and he finally had Lady Luck on his side. An unstop-
pable combination.

He demonstrated his strength in winning the first moun-
tain-top finish to La Rosière and then again on the famous
slopes of the Alpe d'Huez. Along the road to Paris, naturally
there were times when I was disappointed that I wasn't
physically where I needed to be to win my fifth Tour title.
Although at the same time I was filled with happiness for
G and in watching his dream come true.

We all knew that he was capable of doing it, but there
had been some reservations in the team as to whether he
could hold on to his form and good fortune for the full

three weeks. He'd never done it before, but watching him as the race progressed it was clear he was in the shape of his life and it would take a catastrophe to keep him from winning. Several of our rivals on other teams were still not quite treating him as if he was a serious contender; when he attacked from the main group half way up to La Rosière, the final ascent of the day, the others looked at each other and didn't give chase. Whereas every time I accelerated, they were straight on me and wouldn't give me an inch. Despite my own regrets it was a pleasure watching G pulling that off and proving beyond all doubt to everyone that he had the calibre to win a Grand Tour.

The penny had dropped for me on the short, sharp 65-kilometre 17th stage. I followed a move from Primož Roglič on the early slopes of the Col de Portet, the final climb of the day. We were quickly reeled back in by the group of contenders, but I paid for the effort, and I was dropped in the final kilometres. For me that was the moment when it became clear to me that I wouldn't be winning the 2018 Tour. That made it quite simple in the team from then on: it was all about getting 100% behind G, our best shot at winning the race.

I've been there through his journey over the years, back to our rookie days together on Barloworld and then on to Sky, seeing all the little sacrifices, all the low-carb rides we'd done together, all the times we'd get back from training completely nailed. He saw me through my own Tour de France victories, even riding on one year with a fractured pelvis. To have been a part of his journey and ultimate victory will hold a special place in my memory as a professional.

Winning the Tour de France is life-changing, I know that first-hand. There's no other way to put it, and it's something that stays with you for the rest of your life. It's a surreal experience. There's a magic in achieving something you've dreamt of for so long. As I stood next to him on the podium in Paris, I could appreciate how he was feeling. It reminded me how it had been for me, back in 2013 when I won the Tour for the first time.

It had been a special season, winning the Giro d'Italia, then sharing in G's Tour win. Geraint had been there for me over the years. To see him achieve what he did was something we could all enjoy.

Acknowledgements

Thanks to everyone for their help on this journey. To Debbie Wharton and my first club, Maindy Flyers, who helped me fall in love with cycling. To my mum and dad, for steering me in the right direction in those early years, even when I couldn't see it at the time. Dad never pushed me; he said just to give it my best and see what happens, which is something that has always stayed with me. To Darren Tudor, Shane Sutton and everyone at Welsh Cycling for giving me a real taste for what cycling was all about and who really helped kick-start my career. To Rod Ellingworth and everybody in the GB academy. Rod has been one of the biggest influences on my career – not just from a racing perspective, but in teaching me how to be a real professional. And to the Academy boys: Cav, Ed, Swifty, Stannard, Ross Sander and Tennant.

To Matt Parker and Dan Hunt for their help on the Olympic track program. Fran Millar for just being awesome. To Tim Kerrison, my coach, who helped me transition from track to the biggest bike race of all. And a huge thanks to Dave Brailsford, who's been my boss since I was seventeen and who, along with everyone at British Cycling and Sky, has put in place everything I needed to achieve the greatest goal of all.

To our Team Sky sport directors Nico and Servais, my mechanic Diego, soigneurs Marek and Marko, and all the staff, who work flat-out for us over the four weeks across the Tour.

To my teammates at the Tour – not just for their unselfish riding and those three weeks of racing, but for all the hard work that goes in beforehand: Egan Bernal, Jonathan Castroviejo, Chris Froome, Michał Kwiatkowski, Gianni Moscon, Wout Poels and Luke Rowe. A special thanks to Froomey, for never making things tense or awkward.

To my friends in the peloton, who have helped in one way or another throughout my career: Daryl Impey, Steve Cummings, Eddie BH, Bernie Eisel, Mathew Hayman, Richie Porte, Gerro and Robbie Hunter.

To the fans, for all their support on the roadside, on social media and everywhere in between. Your support means a lot. One of the nicest aspects of winning the Tour has been seeing how happy it's made people, young and old, whom I've never met.

To friends and family back home. Eif, Beth, Rhys, Carys and Alys. Ian, Cath, Molly and Jack. Rob and Soph. Dale and Hannah. The Plasmawr gang. Our family in the Valleys, west and north Wales, for all their support, encouragement and understanding.

Luke and everyone at Rocket Sports for their help, encouragement and guidance. A big thanks to Richard Milner and all the team at Quercus, plus David Luxton. It's been as fun as it was the first time around.

To Tom Fordyce for all his hard work getting the book together with me, even when on his family holiday. I really enjoyed reliving it all with him.

And, of course, Sa – for always being there for me, through the tough times as much as the good. Keep living in the moment and enjoying everything. I couldn't have done it without you.

Credits

Plate section images in order of appearance, © and courtesy:

1 – Gareth Enticott
2 – Alamy Stock Photo/Robert Wade
3 – Reuters/Eric Gaillard
4, 5 – Amaury Sport Organisation
6 – Reuters/Benoit Tessier
7, 8, 9, 10, 11, 12, 13, 14, 15, 16, 17, 18 – Russ Ellis
19 – Alamy Stock Photo/Mark Hawkins

Map © and courtesy Bill Donohoe

'The Boy Who Climbed A Mountain' © and courtesy Max Boyce